T0094610

# Shakespeare Made French

## Four Plays
### by
### Jean-François Ducis

# SHAKESPEARE MADE FRENCH

## FOUR PLAYS
## BY JEAN-FRANÇOIS DUCIS

### TRANSLATED
### BY

## MARVIN CARLSON

Martin E. Segal Theatre Center Publications

Frank Hentschker, Executive Director
Rebecca Sheahan, Managing Director

Martin E. Segal Theatre Center Publications
New York, © 2012

All rights reserved. Except for brief passages quoted in newspaper, magazine, radio or television reviews, no part of this book may be reproduced in any form or by any means, electronic or mechanical, including photocopying or recording, or by an information storage and retrieval system, without permission in writing from the publisher.

Professionals and amateurs are hereby warned that this material, being fully protected under the Copyright Laws of the United States of America and all other countries of the Berne and Universal Copyright Conventions, is subject to a royalty. All rights including, but not limited to, professional, amateur, recording, motion picture, recitation, lecturing, public reading, radio and television broadcasting, and the rights of translation into foreign languages are expressly reserved. Inquiries concerning production rights should be addressed in advance, before rehearsals begin, to the Martin E. Segal Theatre Center, 365 5th Avenue, 3rd Floor, New York, NY 10016. Email: mestc@gc.cuny.edu

Library of Congress Cataloging-in-Publication Data

Ducis, J.-F. (Jean-Francois), 1733-1816.
 [Plays. English. Selections]
 Shakespeare made French : four plays / by Jean-Francois Ducis ; translated by Marvin Carlson.
     p. cm.
 Translations of Ducis' adaptations of Shakespeare's four tragedies, which Ducis radically reworked, changing plots, characters and situations to create a Hamlet, a Lear, and others as they might have been conceived by a follower of Racine.
 Translations of Ducis' adaptations of Shakespeare's plays.
 ISBN 978-0-9846160-3-9
 1. Ducis, J.-F. (Jean-Francois), 1733-1816.--Translations into English. 2. Shakespeare, William, 1564-1616.--Adaptations. I. Carlson, Marvin A., 1935- II. Shakespeare, William, 1564-1616. Hamlet. III. Shakespeare, William, 1564-1616. Romeo and Juliette. IV. Shakespeare, William, 1564-1616. King Lear. V. Shakespeare, William, 1564-1616. Othello. VI. Title.
 PQ1981.D6A2 2012
 842'.5--dc23
                    2012023798

Managing Editor, Copy-editing and Layout by
Alexandra Sascha Just
Cover Image Design by Frank Hentschker
Cover Image: "Jean-Francois Ducis Telling the Future of the Actor Talma"
by Louis Ducis, circa 1820, Paris.
Reproduction, oil on canvas, by an anonymous artist.
From the private collection of Marvin Carlson, Ithaca, New York

© 2012 Martin E. Segal Theatre Center

# SHAKESPEARE MADE FRENCH

## FOUR PLAYS
## BY JEAN-FRANÇOIS DUCIS

### TRANSLATED
### BY

## MARVIN CARLSON

MARTIN E. SEGAL
THEATRE CENTER

# TABLE OF CONTENTS

# SHAKESPEARE
# MADE
# FRENCH

# ACKNOWLEDGEMENTS

I would like to thank Sascha Just for her outstanding editorial work as well as Anita Yarbery for her skillful proofreading and Rebecca Sheahan for her exceptional administrative guidance on this project.

Additional thanks to Shane Breaux, Christopher Silsby, and Kalle Westerling for their considerable help with formatting and layout.

Many thanks to Frank Hentschker for supervising the publication and for the cover design.

*To Scott McMillin*

# DUCIS, SHAKESPEARE, AND THE FRENCH

Despite Shakespeare's continuing pre-eminence among Western dramatists not only in the West but around the globe, his significance was long resisted in France, and it was really not until the twentieth century that leading directors in that country, from André Antoine and Firmin Gémier at the outset of the century to late century directors like Daniel Mesguich and Stéphane Braunschweig accepted him as a major dramatist in his own right, without needing serious cutting or accommodation to French traditions and practices. For most of the previous two centuries Shakespeare was regarded usually with condescension and often without outright contempt, at best a talented country bumpkin lacking proper training and at worst a barbarian savage, producing degenerate and obscene work.

The early years of France's exposure to the work of the English dramatist were dominated, in this cultural domain as in many others, by the figure of Voltaire. Shortly before his death in 1778, Voltaire lamented the decline of taste in French culture in general and in theatre in particular, a growing barbarism which was characterized in no small measure by a rapidly growing interest in Shakespeare. "What makes the whole situation even more calamitous and horrible is that fact that I am the one who first mentioned this Shakespeare; I was the first to show the French some pearls that I have found in his enormous dung heap."[1]

Voltaire was not the first critic in France to "mention" Shakespeare, but he was unquestionably the first to call literary attention to him. Sent into England in voluntary exile in 1726, Voltaire remained there two years, a pivotal period in his artistic and political development. His *Lettres philosophiques*, containing extensive observations on England in the 1720s, were published in English in 1733 and in French shortly after. For much of the French intellectual world this was the first detailed information they had about the cultural, social, and political life of their neighbors across the Channel. Two of the essays in this collection were devoted to English comedy and English tragedy, and that on tragedy begins with Shakespeare, whom Voltaire calls the "English Corneille" and the "creator of the English theatre." Here, Voltaire admits Shakespeare's genius, but considers that very genius dangerous because it has led to the widespread imitation in England of his total lack of taste and ignorance of all the rules and proprieties of dramatic art. As an example of the flashes of brilliance, Voltaire cites Hamlet's "to be or not to be" speech, translated into French Alexandrines, but as an example of his crude primitivism, Othello strangling Desdemona in her bed, Roman assassins washing their hands in blood, and the crude and often obscene comic sequences in even the most serious of his plays.

Another French author began calling attention to Shakespeare during these same years. This was the Abbé Prévost, best known today as the author of the novel *Manon Lescault*. Like Voltaire, indeed immediately after him, Prévost spent two years in England (1728 to 1730) and like Voltaire, subsequently reported his impressions of the English drama and especially Shakespeare. His weekly review, *Le Pour et Contre* began publication in 1733, the same year Voltaire's *Lettres philosophiques* was published, and frequently discussed English matter. Shakespeare was given particular attention and Prévost discussed this dramatist at some length at the beginning of 1738. Many subsequent critics have cast Prévost as an ardent defender of Shakespeare against Voltaire's attacks,[2] although as early as 1919 George R. Havens demonstrated by a close reading of the relevant passages that although his tone was softer, Prévost really differed in no substantive way from Voltaire's highly qualified commendation.[3]

With whatever qualifications, however, before mid-century the name Shakespeare was not unfamiliar in French literary circles. This process was unquestionably speeded by the first translations of Shakespearian works, by Pierre-Antoine de La Place, in his four-volume "The English Theatre." Although the collection covered many of the major English dramatists from Shakespeare to the present, Shakespeare was the dominant figure covered and attracted wide-spread attention to La Place's work. The first two volumes, in 1745, included a preface praising Shakespeare's achievement, a biography of the dramatist, and translations of *Othello*, *The Third Part of Henry VI*, *Richard III*, *Hamlet*, and *Macbeth*. So popular were these that they were soon followed by another two, containing *Cymbeline*, *Julius Caesar*, *Antony and Cleopatra*, *Timon of Athens* (as adapted by Thomas Shadwell), and *The Merry Wives of Windsor*. In fact, only in the case of *Richard III* did La Place translate the entire play. For all the rest, he provided narrative bridges between what he considered to be the important scenes. Among other things, these narratives allowed him to essentially omit much of the material that critics like Voltaire and Prévost found crude, indecorous, or inappropriate. He also provided plot summaries of twenty-six other Shakespearian plays, bringing a general acquaintance with the British dramatist's work not only to a much wider French audience, but to readers across Europe. This success clearly irritated Voltaire, not only because La Place replaced him as the leading French authority on the British theatre in general and Shakespeare in particular, but, equally important, because La Place took a much more positive view of Shakespeare's total achievement. From this time onward, Voltaire became a more and more determined opponent of the growing Shakespeare vogue in France.

Diderot and D'Alembert's monumental Encyclopedia, one of the central works of the Enlightenment, appearing from 1751 to 1772, had no specific entry on Shakespeare, but it mentioned him numerous times and, somewhat oddly, included an entry on Stratford which opened with the observation that this town was the birth place of "this sublime genius, the greatest in the history of dramatic poetry."[4] Probably the interest in Stratford and certainly this elevated opinion of Shakespeare owed much to the Parisian visits of David Garrick, the greatest living English actor and one who throughout his career tied his fortunes closely to this author. Garrick first visited Paris briefly in 1751 and even at that time is reported to have dazzled his fellow guests at a dinner party with a rendition of the dagger scene from *Macbeth*.[5] In 1763, when he had built up a network of friends in French social, literary, and theatrical circles, he returned for six months. At this time he was the honored guest at the leading salons in Paris, where he delighted all by his wit, his sophistication, and his impromptu performances of scenes from his favorite author—the dagger scene, which he is reported to have given hundreds of times, as well as Hamlet's "to be or not to be," and a scene of Lear's madness, depicted without words. Just six years before the Shakespeare Jubilee, organized by Garrick in Stratford and a key event in the elevation of Shakespeare from talented playwright to sublime genius, this visit had much to do with the solidification of the dramatist's reputation in France, especially among the creators of the *Encyclopedia,* who met and admired Garrick in these Parisian salons.

By the end of the 1760s there was sufficient interest in Shakespeare to support a production of *Hamlet* at the national theatre, the Comédie Française. Its author was the young Jean-François Ducis, whose only previous work, a neoclassic tragedy, had been a resounding failure. With his *Hamlet*, however, the story was very different. It was received with the greatest enthusiasm. This success was won, however, at considerable cost to the original. Ducis, though an ardent fan of the English author, totally accepted Voltaire's view of Shakespeare as a primitive genius who would have written far different works had he lived in the most delicate, sophisticated, and enlightened atmosphere of classic France. If Ducis had any misgivings about this opinion, he was a shrewd enough dramatist to recognize that the French theatre-going public of his day, however interested they were in Shakespeare, would never accept him on stage in his original form, but only if his works were radically refashioned to conform to the classical French tragic style as it had been developed by Corneille, Racine, and their followers.

Thus came about one of the most odd and yet most successful cultural adaptations in the history of the theatre. The Ducis Shakespearian plays were not translations, and indeed could hardly even be called adaptations. They are complete reworkings of the dramas, to make them compatible with contemporary French practice, a process affecting every element in them, language, metaphor, and verse form, characters and character relationships, themes and action. Nothing perhaps could more illustrate the vast gulf that existed in pre-romantic dramatic practice in France and England than comparing the Ducis Shakespeares with their originals and seeing what has been altered and why in this enormously successful if apparently somewhat perverse project of making a major English dramatist into a French one.

Ducis is notoriously known as being almost completely ignorant of English, but given his project this is not so much of a disadvantage as it might appear. His major source, of course, was the somewhat fragmentary translations of La Place, although by this time there were a number of translated passages of many Shakespearian plays, especially *Hamlet.* Two of Ducis's most popular adaptations, *Hamlet* and *Othello*, appeared in La Place's popular first volume and partial translations or plot summaries were provided by La Place for the other four. La Place's versions were far from accurate, but this was in fact an advantage for Ducis, since in terms of tonality, language, and characters, La Place was already adjusting Shakespeare in the direction that Ducis would develop in much more extreme fashion.

Perhaps the first thing that strikes an English reader in these Ducis tragedies is the reduction and reorientation of characters. There are only eight speaking roles in the Ducis *Hamlet* as opposed to more than twenty in the original. Gone are Laertes and his distracting subplot, Fortinbras, the Ghost,

Rosencrantz and Guildenstern, and of course the gravediggers with their unacceptable comic tone and their even more unacceptable puns and word play. The remaining roles are almost evenly divided, as in Racine, between major characters and their faithful followers, or *confidants,* who generally have little to do on their own but essentially serve as foils to provide dialogue with their superior masters. Thus Hamlet, who is here the King, has a confidant, Norceste, a pale shadow of Horatio, Gertrude has a confidante Elvire, and Polonius is pressed into service as co-conspirator with and confidant of Claudius, who with the support of Gertrude murdered Hamlet's father and now plots against Hamlet himself to gain the throne. Ophelia is not the daughter of Polonius, but of Claudius, and thus, as Hamlet becomes aware of Claudius' crimes he is torn, in typically French neoclassic fashion, between his love for Ophelia and his hatred of her father. The final character is Voltimand, captain of the guards, who serves basically as a general utility figure.

The second feature to strike the reader is Ducis's language. Ever since the beginning of the classic period, serious French drama was invariably composed in Alexandrines, rhymed couplets of twelve syllables each, with strict rules as to their rhyme schemes and internal divisions. Not until romantics like Victor Hugo was this traditional verse form challenged and Ducis is scrupulous in its use, as his audiences would have inspected. The present translation uses the more familiar, and more Shakespearian ten-syllable iambic pentameter, but keeps the French rhymed couplets to indicate the strongly patterned rhythm of the original. A less obvious feature of Ducis's language is its reliance on words and expressions that by his time had become standard on the French classic stage, words like "Heaven" and "vengeance," rather abstract and familiar from the tradition, instead of the rich and innovative language and metaphor of Shakespeare. Word play and puns, so beloved by Shakespeare, were totally unacceptable.

Naturally, the plays had to follow the famous "three unities" of the neoclassic drama—time, place, and action. Thus, insofar as possible, all of the plays emphasize a rather general and undefined location, either indoors as in *Hamlet,* whose vague antechamber looks backward to the many similar spaces in Racine, or outdoors, as in *Lear,* where rough crags and rugged forests look forward to the romantic theatre. The time is as close as possible to the single day insisted upon in neoclassic practice, so that all of *Hamlet*, for example, takes place on the day selected for Hamlet's coronation, and all the manipulations of Claudius and Polonius, long prepared, are directed toward disrupting that event. The unity of action involves removing all subplots, and when possible, the characters, like Laertes, involved in them. Obviously then, *Hamlet* contains no duel, but violence of that sort would be unacceptable onstage in any case, and physical conflicts, like deaths, are covered, according to classic practice, by *récits,* modeled on the messenger speeches of Greek tragedy.

Like all the Shakespeare enthusiasts of his generation, Ducis looked to Garrick as the greatest living authority on that dramatist. He kept engravings of the dramatist and of the actor in the role of *Hamlet* on his writing table, and not long before the opening of his *Hamlet* reworking in Paris, he wrote to Garrick explaining the adjustments he had been forced to make to the text to satisfy

French expectations. Among the "savage irregularities" which he had been thus forced to reject, he cited "the acknowledged ghost who speaks interminably, the strolling players, and the dueling scene."[6]

Ducis had hope that the leading actor of the Comédie, Lekain, would create his Othello, but Lekain, a protegé of Voltaire, would have nothing to do with Shakespeare. Therefore the first French Hamlet was François-René Molé, then a lesser but still a leading figure at the theatre. It was clear from the outset that Ducis had successfully responded to the tastes of his audience. The play remained popular throughout the Shakespeare frenzy of the romantic period and was repeated 203 times by 1851, making it the most popular new offering of the century. Among Ducis's contemporaries, only Voltaire could boast any comparable success. The influence of French theatre and French taste was such that in many parts of Europe Ducis's Hamlet was known before Shakespeare's. Such was the case in Spain, which saw no less than four translations of Ducis's play beginning in 1772, in Italy, in the Low Countries, Poland, and Russia.[7]

The enormous success of the Ducis Hamlet also stimulated further interest in staging the English dramatist's works in France, though, of course, in highly modified form. The very year after Hamlet, Mme. d'Epinay commissioned the young Chevalier de Chastellux (later to play an important role in the American Revolution) to create a Roméo et Juliette, which enjoyed a great success even though presented by a company of amateurs. A rather sardonic letter from Mme. Riccoboni, who was present, to Garrick suggests how far Chastellux still was from the original: "Instead of occupying themselves with poisoning each other and stabbing each other, Juliet and Romeo gaily depart from this funereal retreat to marry who knows where and to live together who knows how and to be happy in any way you can imagine."[8]

The Chastellux event was widely discussed in Parisian cultural circles and may well have contributed to Ducis's decision to follow the success of his Hamlet with this tragedy of youthful lovers in 1772. Indeed, Ducis may well have had access to the Chastellux version, since otherwise his most likely source would have been La Place, who provides only a general summary of the play's action. In fact the Ducis version is almost equally far from Chastellux as from Shakespeare. Avoiding the happy ending that Mme. Riccoboni found so ludicrous, he not only allowed his lovers to die, but to do so on stage, and further, to defy unity of place in order to show their mutual tomb.

Again the Shakespearian action and characters are much reduced. Flavia, a colorless confidante, replaces the gossiping nurse. Characters like Tybalt, Mercutio, and the Friar disappear entirely. The family feud still sets the ground of the action, but it is driven entirely by the mad thirst for revenge of old Montague and to justify the extremity of his passion, Ducis goes outside Shakespeare to Dante and the grim story of Ugolino, forced in captivity to devour his own sons. Somewhat surprisingly, this element of gothic horror[9] aroused little protest, the audience being more troubled by the onstage death of the lovers. In response to substantial audience protest, Ducis created a variant happy ending, but even so, the play was only a modest success, and had a far less impressive career than Hamlet, though it was revived four times during the next thirteen years, for a total of thirty-eight performances.[10]

When Ducis returned to Shakespeare eleven years later, in 1783, with *Le Roi Léar,* the world of French Shakespeare had been radically changed by the appearance of a twenty-volume translation of the English dramatist's plays by Pierre Le Tourneur. The first volume appeared in 1776, four years after Ducis's *Roméo and Juliette,* and the final one in 1782, the year before his *Léar.* Le Tourneur's project far surpassed that of La Place in almost every way. The La Place translations, though of much interest to the French aristocracy, had no official support, and indeed not even a royal permission to publish. As a result, it appeared anonymously and with a false London imprint. The Le Tourneur volumes were a very different matter. The edition was launched by a subscription list of almost a thousand members, including high ranking members of the court, the army, the church, as well as ambassadors, academicians, and such foreign subscribers as Catherine of Russia, King George III, the Prince of Wales, and the Archbishop of Canterbury. By special royal permission, the edition was dedicated to the young Louis XVI. The appearance of the first two volumes in 1776, which contained *Othello, Julius Caesar*, and *The Tempest,* was a major European event. The preface, praising Shakespeare as the world's greatest dramatic genius, elevating him above Corneille and Racine, and not even mentioning Voltaire, not surprisingly solidified Voltaire's opposition to Shakespeare, which continued unabated for the rest of his life. Typical was his comment in a public letter to his friend d'Argental, a subscriber to the project, written only three months after the appearance of the first two volumes: "I was the first to show to the French some pearls that I had found in his enormous dung heap. I did not expect that this would serve one day to trample underfoot the crowns of Racine and Corneille in order to adorn the brow of a barbarian mountebank."[11] Later that same year Voltaire had a paper read before the French Academy, recalling that the ongoing mission of that body was to preserve French literary standards, a task that demanded now that they take a stand against the corrupting influence of Shakespeare.

Such declarations from the leading defender of the neoclassic tradition did little to stem the tide. The Le Tourneau project inexorably continued. Volumes 3 and 4, in 1778, added *Coriolanus, Macbeth, Cymbeline*, and *Romeo and Juliet.* This same year, Voltaire died, all too aware that his campaign to keep French literature from the contamination of Shakespeare had clearly failed. Fortunately, he could not have known that his chair at the prestigious French Academy was upon his death awarded to Ducis, a choice that probably would have enraged him far more than anything the Shakespearian campaign had so far achieved. The following year Le Tourneur's project continued with *Lear and Hamlet*, sharing volume 5, and so on through the twentieth volume in 1782. This was followed the next year by a new Ducis Shakespeare at the national theatre, *Le Roi Léar.* In a dedicatory epistle to the King, Le Tourneur promised that his translations would "free Shakespeare from the paste diamonds that have been substituted for his true riches," and provide at last "an exact and truly faithful translation." The difference from La Place was indeed striking. Here were no summaries or selected passages, but complete plays, and when Le Tourneur adjusted particular words or phrases to accord better with French tragic style or softened crude or obscene material, the translator attempted to explain his adjustments in copious notes offering more literal variations.

Thus by the time Ducis turned his attention to *King Lear,* he had available a far more accurate and detailed translation than had been available to him in his previous Shakespearian works. Indeed, his preface to the play credits Le Tourneur as a major source. In fact, however, the demands of the neoclassic stage tradition far outweighed any considerations to produce a work closer to the original. To begin with, Le Tourneur's translations were all in prose, which would not have been tolerated on the serious French stage until well into the next century. Ducis was not totally orthodox in unity of place, but still required only two locations, not far apart, instead of the many, covering a wide area, in Shakespeare. Unity of time was better observed, as was unity of action. The elaborate Gloucester subplot disappeared, along with its totally unacceptable blinding, and the named characters reduced to twelve, in fact quite a large number of a neoclassic tragedy. Obviously the Fool, with his questionable tonality, was eliminated, and Goneril (here Volnérille) is often mentioned, but never appears. The sons of Gloucester, now Edgar and Lénox, become sons of Kent, faithful and patriotic followers of Lear and suitors of Cordelia, here Helmonde. The Dover scene and much of the madness (including Poor Tom) disappears, though Ducis's Lear, more pathetic than truly mad, does suffer through a considerable storm. The play ends happily, with Lear, reason restored, united with his loving daughter. Ducis has a typical eighteenth century fondness for the sentimental, particularly when it involves troubled relationships between fathers and daughters. This was already an important emotional element in *Hamlet* and in *Roméo et Juliette* and was of course central to *Le Roi Léar*. Ducis felt that the clearest evidence for the "happy" choice of this piece was the flowing of his own tears during its composition and of those of the audience afterward. He urged fathers to rake their daughters for their moral improvement, and indeed is reported to have carried his own daughters to a performance of the work. On this occasion the playwright, whose reputation for mildness was notable, is reported to have remarked: "If they had not dissolved in tears, I would have strangled them with my bare hands."[12] The play had a success roughly comparable to that of *Roméo et Juliette,* with four revivals during the following decade, and a total of thirty-seven performances.

In all, Ducis created six Shakespearian works, four of which, those in this collection, enjoyed either moderate or considerable success. *Macbeth,* presented in 1784, one year after *Léar,* with the support of the great actor of the era, Talma, was revived as late as 1804, but actually still had only four revivals, for a total of twenty-eight performances. Ducis's next such work, *Jean Sans-Terre*, drawn from *King John,* was an outright failure, presented only seven times in 1791 and never revived. *Macbeth* follows the general procedures already well established by Ducis's earlier works. Secondary characters are eliminated and the lines of action simplified. Banquo disappears, and the ghost that appears to Macbeth is that of Duncan, who disrupts not a banquet but Macbeth's coronation. Themes familiar to Ducis and indeed to late eighteenth century drama in general, such as the benevolence of kindly nature in contrast to the evils of civilized life and the return of the lost and/or adopted son, were all present, here centered on Duncan's son Malcolm, the pure child raised in the hills who returns to claim his throne when the remorseful Macbeth kills himself. The play's real villain is Lady Macbeth, converted into Frédegonde. It was the supernatural elements that gave Ducis the most trouble. The Ghost, studiously avoided on the traditional French tragic stage and by Ducis himself in his *Hamlet* he here allowed to appear, but he was forced to draw the line at the witches. In their place appears a strange luminal character, Iphyctone, perhaps modeled on the classical Tiresias, who is identified as the "minister and interpreter of the gods." The witches themselves are heard offstage in one of the many variants Ducis provided for possible producers of the play according to how willing they were to move beyond strict classic practice. This use of variants to come closer to the original Ducis doubtless learned from the Le Tourneur translations, but in his case the strategy did not win over much support for the play. Although he totally reworked it in 1790, it never gained much popularity.

Ducis's next work, eight years after *Macbeth,* appeared in a far different world. In 1789, the fall of the Bastille marked the beginning of the French Revolution and the beginning of the end of the social world and the theatre world which had shaped the Ducis adaptations. As the country became more and more politically divided, this division literally split apart the national theatre, the majority of the older actors not surprisingly supporting the aristocratic regime that had been their principle sponsors and the majority of the younger actors siding with the new revolutionary movement. Tensions grew and during the Easter closing of 1791; the younger members withdrew from the company to form a rival theatre, the Nation, clearly more sympathetic to the Revolution. Ducis, a major dramatist of the old Comédie, might have been expected to remain with them, but his sympathies were with the departing party and he was a close friend of their leader, François-Joseph Talma, who now became the chief interpreter of Ducis's works, his former leading man, Molé, having remained behind with the conservative group.

This was a fortunate change for Ducis, since Talma soon became the leading actor of France, a position he retained until his death in 1826. He took over Ducis's previous leading roles, particularly excelling as Hamlet, and premiered Ducis's final Shakespeares at the new Nation theatre. Not even the talents of Talma, however, could make a success of *Jean Sans-Terre* in 1792, a few months after the opening of the new theatre. This was unquestionably the weakest of Ducis's Shakespearian works, and soon disappeared from the stage. This is the only Ducis Shakespeare with a substantive subtitle, a clear guide to its content. The subtitle is "The Death of Arthur," and indeed that event, a single incident in Shakespeare's play, taking up only about 300 lines, has been expanded to Ducis's full drama which, uniquely for this author, consists of only three acts. Falconbridge is missing, as is Eleanor, the English earls, all of the French characters, and indeed any mention of a war. The entire action takes place in the Tower of London, and consists mostly of the vain attempts of Hubert to save Arthur and his laments afterward when he is unable to do so. John is an unmitigated villain, who kills both Arthur and Constance, in conventional fashion offstage. Although the work faithfully follows classic practice, it is neither particularly successful as a traditional tragedy and it is the furthest from the original of any of the Ducis's adaptations. Its failure is hardly surprising.

Ducis fared much better with his final adaptation, *Othello* in 1792, not only because it was a richer and more fully realized drama than the truncated *Jean,* but probably equally important, because it provided a strong role for Talma, who enjoyed a great success in it. Revived four times in the next two decades, through the darkest years of the Terror, it achieved fifty-four performances, distinctly surpassing any of the other Ducis adaptations except *Hamlet.* The action takes place entirely in Venice, though in three separate locations. Ducis reduced the cast to eight, about half of them, as usual, confidants, although, of course, Shakespeare had provided him with two figures ready made for such conversion—Iago and Emilia. Both required much thinning out to reduce them to the confidant role, but in Iago this was essential, as the original was far too monstrous, in Ducis's opinion, to be tolerated by a French public. Pézare, who replaces Iago, is thus not only less deeply evil than Iago, but Ducis took care to keep his evil "carefully hidden" from the spectators "until the very end of the action."[13] Othello's skin also had to be lightened for this sensitive public. Says Ducis: "I thought that the yellow coppery tine would have the advantage of not revolting the eye of the public, and especially that of the women."[14]

Ducis's plot follows Shakespeare in broad outlines, but the differences in detail are enormous. While Iago is diminished into the rather feckless Pézare, Cassio is developed into a central character, Lorédan, son of the Doge, who plays a variety of not entirely consistent roles, the would-be lover of Hédelmone (Desdemona), the object of Othello's suspicion, and at last the noble youth who despite his very real passion for the heroine, steps aside in favor of Othello, her true love. Whether this sacrifice is successful or not depends upon which version of the place is utilized. Originally Ducis followed Shakespeare and allowed the distraught and deceived Othello to kill Desdemona and himself on stage. This bold ending, Ducis reports, made a "terrible" impression. The audience arose as one man in protest and several women fainted.[15] The obliging author at once created an alternative ending, subsequently used with success, in which an unlikely crowd pours into the bedroom at the critical moment, reveals the manipulations of Pézare, the misunderstandings of Othello, and the purity of the saved Hédelmone. As usual, almost every adjustment is made to suit the actual or imagined sensitivities of a neoclassically trained audience. A particularly striking example of this is the handkerchief. "Mouchoir" was clearly a low-class term totally unacceptable on the tragic stage, and so Ducis converts the object used against his heroine to a "diamond headband" given her by Othello, a suitably heroic ornament. His prudence was shown by the uproar generated in 1829 when Alfred de Vigny, in his *More de Venise,* utilized this word, to the scandal of both actors and audience, for the first time in the history of the French tragic theatre. Even de Vigny did not have the temerity to mention that the handkerchief was decorated with strawberries (*fraises*), a word even lower-class than "mouchoir." His handkerchief was "decorated with Oriental flowers." It was another hundred years, well into the twentieth century, before Desdemona's strawberries were mentioned on the French stage.[16]

Such delicacy seems almost impossible to believe in a public which less than two months before had witnessed and on the whole applauded the September Massacres and were on the brink of the most notorious period of the

French Revolution, the Reign of Terror. Ducis, who despite the fearful material in his plays, was a mild and gentle spirit, went into seclusion as the social situation worsened. When a friend chided him after the great success of *Othello* for giving up his career when his fame was at its peak, he replied "Why talk to me, Vallier, of composing tragedies? Tragedy walks the streets. If I put my foot out of doors, I have blood up to my ankle."[17]

Ducis's reputation continued strong and several of his works survived well into the next century. Most notably, the young Sarah Bernhardt achieved her first success in serious drama playing Helmonde in Ducis's *Roi Léar* at the Odéon in 1867. With the triumph of Romanticism in the French theatre in the 1830s however Ducis's approach was increasingly and properly seen as the work of another era and another sensibility. The romantics openly acknowledged Shakespeare as their model and patron saint, and insisted upon (though with mixed success, especially in early attempts like that of de Vigny) a Shakespeare as free as possible from the expectations of the neoclassic tradition. The Ducis project, to create a Shakespeare that would be accessible to and acceptable to an audience trained in and sympathetic to that tradition, was regarded as a foolish and misguided, at best somewhat curious eccentricity of the now-discarded old regime.

Without attempting to see Ducis as a major dramatic poet, which he clearly was not, we can today, I think, view his work in more positive terms, as a particularly interesting and on the whole successful example of the sort of intercultural mixing that today, as our consciousness becomes more global, is an increasingly important part of our study of how theatre changes in moving among cultures. Within the European tradition in the late eighteenth century, it would have been difficult to find dramatic approaches more antithetical than the English, primarily represented by Shakespeare, and the French, primarily represented by Racine. The project of attempting to reconceive one in the style of the other seems almost unimaginable, and yet Ducis managed to accomplish this, with considerable success. His works are unlikely to re-establish themselves on the stage, but they endure as fascinating studies of the dynamics of intercultural theatre.

— Marvin Carlson
New York City, October 2012

## ENDNOTES

1. July 19, 1776. *Correspondence.*
2. Among the most recent John Pemble in *Shakespeare Goes to Paris* (Hambledon and London: London, 2005), which characterizes Prévost's reading of Shakespeare as "eulogistic" (4).
3. G.R. Havens, "The Abbé Prévost and Shakespeare" in *Modern Philology* 17:4 (August, 1919), 177-98.
4. Louis de Jaucourt, "Stratford" in the *Encyclopédie ou Dictionnaire raisonné des sciences, des arts et des métiers* 15 (Paris: Braisson, 1765), 541.
5. Frank A. Hedgecock, *A Cosmopolitan Actor: David Garrick and His French Friends* (London: Stanley Paul, 1912 ), 108.
6. April 14, 1769, David Garrick, *The Private Correspondence*, ed. James Boaden, 2 vol. (London, Colburn, 1832), 2:560.
7. Angel Luis Pujante, "The Four Neoclassical Spanish Hamlets: Assimilation and Revision," *Sederi* (2005), 121, n. 1, (Paris: SFELT, 1947).
8. P. van Tieghem, *Découverte de Shakespeare sur le continent*, 234.
9. Or "visigothic" according to Voltaire. *Oeuvres completes* (Paris: Renouard, 1819-23), 86:3.
10. Production records of the Ducis adaptations in this essay are taken from the appendix to John Golder's *Shakespeare for the Age of Reason* (Oxford: Voltaire Foundation, 1992), by far the most comprehensive study of the Ducis Shakespeare works.
11. Voltaire, *Oeuvres*, 94:204.
12. E. Preston Dargan, "Shakespeare and Ducis" in *Modern Philology,* 10:2 (Oct., 1912), 156.
13. Jean-François Ducis, "*Avertissement to Othello*" in *Oeuvres* 2 (Paris: Ne preu, 1826), 171.
14. Ibid., 169.
15. Ibid.
16. Pemble, *Shakespeare Goes to Paris*, 105-6.
17. J. J. Jusserand, *Shakespeare in France* (London: Unwin, 1889), 436.

# HAMLET

## 1769

## Cast of Characters

Claudius

Polonius

Gertrude

Hamlet

Ophelia

Elvire

Norceste

Voltimand

Conspirators

# ACT I

## Scene 1

### CLAUDIUS, POLONIUS

CLAUDIUS:     Polonius, the time draws on apace
When Hamlet must go and I assume his place,
This idle prince, committed as it seems,
To drifting in his solitary dreams.
Norceste, of whom I have the most to fear,
Supports him, but he is no longer here.
Rumors abound that he'll return some day
But rumors they remain. He stays away.
His zeal for Hamlet I have often noted
And frankly fear a subject so devoted;
But I have strong supporters of my own,
Armed and prepared to place me on the throne.

POLONIUS:     Your followers are valiant, it is true,
And totally subservient to you.
Under your leadership they cannot fail
To conquer all and make your side prevail.

CLAUDIUS:     My speech to them just now inflamed their zeal
"Friends," I began, "like me I know you feel
Deeply the loss of our lamented king
Whose death you know is threatening to bring
Fear and confusion to our threatened state
Whose happiness was hitherto so great.
The memory of his victorious reign
Makes more dark still the future and its pain.
His passing Heaven marked with storms severe
Freezing our hearts as we knelt down in fear.
'Tis said that when the final breath he took
The oceans raged, the earth's foundations shook."
I called to mind the fearful storm that started
The very moment that our liege departed.
When rivers burst untrammeled from the bed
And graves burst open to expose the dead
The ocean depths their darkest secrets showed
While over all the lightning flashed and glowed.
Few ships survived, and town and farm alike

Reeled helpless under Heaven's ruthless strike.
The suffering Danes, their terror at its height
Witnessed God's power and trembled at the sight.
To some the dead king's ghost seemed to appear;
Some cried in fright while others froze in fear.
It was as if the gates of hell did gape
And usher forth this fierce and armed shape.
As if the gods benevolence forswore
And shook the earth's foundations to its core.
And as I spoke, their faces all betrayed
The grim impression these events had made.
The human spirit counts for little when
Confronting something far beyond its ken.
So I continued: "Surely such upheaval
In Nature augurs great impending evil.
These Northern lands are full of well-armed foes
Ready to strike whenever weakness shows.
A monarch's death may well precipitate
Perilous times for the most stable state.
Now that his reign is over, I concede
That he was truly virtuous indeed.
Although despite my services I must
Complain to me he often was unjust.
His cruelty and arrogance extended
To my dear daughter, and it ended
By isolating her and making sure
A proper mate she never would secure.
Thus out of jealousy he made it sure
My house and heritage would not endure.
Despite all this, a greater threat we face
In that weak son he left us in his place.
Morose and melancholy, disinclined
To show initiative of any kind
Whose idle life so far has not revealed
The virtue that is tested on the field.
He has performed no deeds of high renown
To glorify his family and the crown.
What can I say? His reason is unstable,
Fixed on some fantasy, often unable
To act at all, then, on a whim
Calm passes and some madness seizes him.
From such a ruler, what can be expected?
Of course our envious neighbors have detected

Our weakness and look forward to the day
When they, united, sweep us all away.
What powerful arm, made strong and firm in war,
Can stem the tide they are preparing for?
By what right then can I take on this role?
By toppling this weak and hapless soul,
A shadow of a king, whose every breath
In drawn in lassitude, fit but for death.
By blood and boldness, it is plain to see
I am by far more fit to rule than he."
So spoke I, and with thunderous applause,
All those who heard me rallied to my cause.
In short, so overwhelming was my case
That I was hailed as king, in Hamlet's place.
I now dare hope that I've inaugurated
A movement that will grow and not be sated
Till Hamlet is disgraced and overthrown
And eager hands uplift me to his throne.
Moreover I have worked behind the scenes
To work for this event by darker means
By spreading rumors, false but laced with truth
About the weaknesses of Hamlet's youth,
By emphasizing these I have been able
To plant at large the thought he is unstable.
The people and the army have surmised
Even his virtue has been compromised.
These are the evil seeds that I have sown
And now am posed to harvest what they've grown.

POLONIUS:    It may well be your victory depends
More on those rumors than upon your friends.
What are your plans? The Queen seems quite inclined
In you the marks of sovereign to find.
Though she is bound to follow every letter
Of protocol, when all are feeling better
To offer to her people some relief
From this exhausting pouring out of grief.
She then will turn to you and you must be
Prepared for that eventuality.
Accept her love, and clasp her to your side.
Don't hesitate, for wrath and wounded pride
Might cause her to reflect upon your past
And all your plots might be revealed at last.

CLAUDIUS:     I'm well ahead of you. I am indeed
              Prepared to wed her. More, she has agreed.

POLONIUS:     She has!

CLAUDIUS:                     With this bold stroke I can erase
              All my dark secrets, leaving not a trace.
              Since the King's death, her spirits have declined,
              Her fears have grown. She's troubled in her mind.
              Perhaps I wrong her, but she seems to fear
              Public appearances with me too near.
              Whenever dealing with her I must act
              With utmost subtlety and utmost tact,
              Give in to all her whims, whenever I think
              She's standing on some precipice's brink.
              That's rare, however. Her credulity
              Insures she keeps nothing concealed from me.
              But I should tell you, friend, I fear the most
              Not stories of the King's returning ghost,
              Nor bolts of lightning, nor tempestuous seas,
              Great fires, or other portents such as these.
              I hardly think immortal gods would deign
              To mark with such display some mortal's reign
              Or through the universe into upheaval
              Because of some small passing human evil.
              Ah no, the gods' displeasure never harms me;
              It is an earthly danger than alarms me.
              Hamlet despises me, for all his dreaming.
              And I have no idea what he's scheming.
              He has some secret hidden deep inside.

POLONIUS:     To solve his mystery I've often tried,
              Since his presumed indifference I feel
              Masks some deep anguish that he must conceal.
              He is a quiet soul, but not at rest;
              A heart on fire beats within his breast.
              What he is feeling he will never show
              And Heaven knows how deep those feelings go.
              His melancholy glance is sometimes cast
              On fair Ophelia, but that's quickly past.
              He turns toward heaven, seeking some relief
              From what appears to be unceasing grief.
              Although their outlines yet remain obscure,

Great passions stir within him, I am sure,
And they will surface. Do not be misled.
They won't be pacified 'til they are fed.
Moreover, if I know his heart at all
Hamlet has now begun to hear their call.
"Recall your virtuous father!" they have pleaded,
"Who gave his subjects everything they needed.
Just and courageous, only doing ill
To evil folk. Would he were reigning still!"
Move quickly then. Your plans are all in place.
Delay's the greatest peril that we face.
It's time to call our friends to mobilize.
The moment has arrived to seize the prize.
Don't hesitate, commit what crimes we must,
Final success makes every action just.

CLAUDIUS:    I hear a noise. Leave us. It is the Queen.
I don't know why. Still, you need not be seen.
Go, but not far, for I must speak with her
And when she has departed we'll confer.


Scene 2

CLAUDIUS *and* GERTRUDE

CLAUDIUS:    At last, Madam, that happy day is here
When I can love, and need no longer fear.
I know that until now, your husband gone
The State has had to lean on you alone.
Your tender care, as long as peace endured,
The comfort of your citizens assured.
But now war threatens, and no longer
Can woman rule, the State needs someone stronger.
The troops need leadership, joining our hands
Will authorize me as the time demands.
The torches are prepared to celebrate
Our nuptials, and we need no longer wait.

GERTRUDE:    I would have thought, Sir, prudence would restrain
Your bold impatience, but I hoped in vain.
When all my people are still plunged in grief
At losing their beloved king and chief,

His ashes having scarcely been interred
In the dark romb, what could be more absurd
And more outrageous to my sorrowing nation
Than calling for a wedding celebration?
Consider the impression it would make
A wedding festival to undertake.
Many mistrust your motives, and it's clear
We must do nothing to increase their fear.

CLAUDIUS:  What madness! Is it possible you're cowed
By the opinions of the vulgar crowd?
What business have they with affairs of state?
Your argument may bear a certain weight,
But common rules of action can't confine
Such elevated souls as yours and mine.
In royal weddings, what the State requires
Surpasses any personal desires.
Cease frivolous excuses. I relied
Upon your word that you would be my bride.
On that I based my hope, my joy, my trust.
Are you now wavering?

GERTRUDE:                              No, Sir, but I must,
In my defense, make my misgivings clear,
And speak my mind directly, without fear.
You know the price we've paid to gain our goal—
That memory will always haunt my soul.
The horror we committed still, I find,
Waking or sleeping, occupies my mind.
Do not presume that you can show me how
To turn my thoughts to love or marriage now.
Those hopes are gone, and they will not return;
Repentance now should be our sole concern.
The truth is clear and we cannot ignore it.
We both have sinned and we must suffer for it.
There is a power above us which is just.
I tremble, but I realize we must
Endure the punishment that power brings
On those who topple its annointed kings.

CLAUDIUS:  Madam, your pain is honest, I can see
But I respectfully must disagree.
That crime which now arouses such misgiving

Seemed not so heinous when the King was living.
Perhaps you have forgotten how your Lord
Refused to give my service due reward.
When on the battlefield I saved the nation,
He gave me nothing but humiliation.
Scorned everything I did until my name
Became a symbol of disgrace and shame.
He was suspicious of us, too, you know,
Preparing in his hate some fatal blow
To bring me down, I'm sure, and, who can tell
Perhaps depriving you of life as well.
Moody and jealous, keeping you in dread,
Cruel and hateful ...

GERTRUDE:                                 Stop! Now he is dead.
He was my husband. I must not deprive him
Of those good memories that may survive him.
In any case, his deeds cannot excuse
Our act. We must repent and not accuse.
Ambition blinded me, but now the light
Of sweet repentance has restored my sight.
Life's flickering flame burns low and will resume
Its glow at last when I approach my tomb.
The most intrepid women turn aside
Confronted with the act of parricide.
If he anticipated my design
And sought to block it, still the guilt is mine.
I've bared to you my soul, where you may see
To what extent remorse has vanquished me.
Though my despair I've taken pains to hide,
Be sure that I am trembling inside.
Ambition never tempted me at all.
If lust for power held me in its thrall
Why wouldn't I, if such was my desire
Pass over you, and with my son conspire?
Perhaps some other woman with more pride
Than I possess would rally to your side
And cause by bold exploits and strenuous labors
Denmark to be applauded by its neighbors.
That goal's not mine, and I would rather view
My dear son on the throne, my Lord, than you.
I'll strive to cure his morbid introspection
And give him and my people my protection.

I'll nourish in my breast a contrite feeling
I'll call on Nature to effect my healing.
I pity you, and call you to decide
If in that state you'd take me as a bride.
Conspirators much keep each other guessing;
I find all this duplicity distressing.
Henceforth I am devoted to the path
Of piety, avoiding Heaven's wrath.

CLAUDIUS:     Your feelings, Madame, cannot bring you blame.
I frankly vow my thoughts are much the same.
But can you think your son is a solution?
Consider his lethargic constitution.
Just think of what the monarchy demands.
Would you put all that power in his hands?
And if at last the people couldn't bear
His rule and rose against him ...

GERTRUDE:                                        Who would dare?
Your own allegiance surely would be ample
To serve for all as model and example.
And if some individual rebelled,
You'd see to it at once his threat was quelled.

CLAUDIUS:     But still ...

GERTRUDE:                          Enough. I have no fear.
My son's high qualities will soon appear.
The gods, who surely hear my contrite prayers
Will sooth his torments, pacify his cares.
His father taken by my crime, I must
Be mother to him, it is only just.
(A GUARD appears.)
Guard, call Polonius, tell him I await
His coming, to discuss affairs of state.
(The GUARD leaves. to CLAUDIUS)
And you're aware Sir, how much it must mean
To me, to act as I must, as the Queen.

## Scene 3

### CLAUDIUS, GERTRUDE, POLONIUS

GERTRUDE:    Polonius, I wish without delay
To have my Hamlet crowned. Make it today!
Name him at once the sovereign of our nation.
(POLONIUS *leaves.*)
And you, my Lord, must lead the celebration.
Don't be offended, I have no desire
To cause you shame or to incite your ire.
I know that love alone caused our offense
But Hamlet's suffering was the consequence.
I listened to you, now you must to me,
Become his subject, pledge your fealty.
Prove your remorse by this and thus restore
The virtue that you once so proudly bore.
The gods' laws we must hear and understand,
Keeping secure our kings, as they command.
Go, leave me.


## Scene 4

### GERTRUDE

GERTRUDE:                      Free at last! Now I can bring
Happiness to my son, our future king.
At last my long-distracted heart can find
That tenderness for which it was designed.
Give him my love, of which he was deprived ...


## Scene 5

### ELIVIRE, GERTRUDE

ELVIRE:    Madam, the Lord Noceste has just arrived.

GERTRUDE:    Norceste! What joy! How we have suffered since
We last laid eyes on that most virtuous Prince.
What brings him back from England, do you know?
His presence is a balm for all my woe!

ELVIRE:        Before he left your son and he had grown
               Into the closest friends I've ever known.
               Norceste is rightly praised; he is a youth
               Of virtue, pledged to honor and to truth.
               Your son and he have found in conversation
               A mutual tenderness and admiration.
               Despite his absence, surely Norceste still
               Is trusted by your son. Perhaps he will
               Reveal unto his friend that secret woe
               That he's forbidden all of us to know.

GERTRUDE:      You think he will?

ELVIRE:                                    It's what I would have guessed.

GERTRUDE:      You raise new hope within this mother's breast.
               But if my son should die and never tell
               His secret, that will mean my death as well.

# ACT II

## Scene 1

### ELVIRE, GERTRUDE

ELVIRE:
Madame, your suffering is plain to see.
What are you hiding? Please, confide in me,
Madame.

GERTRUDE:
                              Leave me, I pray.

ELVIRE:
                                                    What do you fear?
Today before your court you must appear.
All are preparing for the coronation ...

GERTRUDE:
I hardly can control my agitation.
I would support my son with all my heart
But a dark horror still holds back a part.
A mortal fear will not depart my mind.

ELVIRE:
I've long suspected something of the kind.

GERTRUDE:
You have suspected? Speak! What do you mean?

ELVIRE:
Perhaps no other witnesses have seen ...

GERTRUDE:
What have you seen, Elvire? Tell me, please!

ELVIRE:
Must I reveal your own dark mysteries?

GERTRUDE:
What have you seen? Reveal it.

ELVIRE:
                                                    I suppose
A guilty secret holds you in its throes.

GERTRUDE:
Apparently I can no more conceal
My sin.

ELVIRE:
                              You tremble.

GERTRUDE:
                                                    Never mind. Reveal
What you suspect.

ELVIRE:                    You force me then?

GERTRUDE:                                              I do.
Open your heart to me, I order you.

ELVIRE:           When murder struck our King that fateful night,
You fled at once from everybody's sight
Seeming to wish no witness to your tears.
But I pursued you, stricken by vague fears,
And found you, not with wifely grief transfixed
But torn by passions curiously mixed.
What did I witness? Overflowing eyes,
Of course, but midst that weeping, curious cries
Of agony and pleas for death, the source
Of which seemed something like remorse.
"How could I? My own husband!" You cried out.

GERTRUDE:       I said that?

ELVIRE:                      Yes. What was all that about?
You're trembling.

GERTRUDE:                    No, I'm dying.

ELVIRE:                                        You admit ...

GERTRUDE:       Leave me!

ELVIRE:                    His death ...

GERTRUDE:                                      I was to blame for it!

ELVIRE:           Your husband! Heavens!

GERTRUDE:                          Fly from me, Elvire!
The very air I breath infects you here.
Go now!

ELVIRE:                          Detested court! Some monster there
Led you to the calamity!

GERTRUDE:                          Beware,
Elvire, of love's dark power. Learn from my plight

How all our sex is threatened by its might
From earliest youth. When Claudius I saw,
At once I loved him, following Heaven's law.
We hid, of course, our mutual affection.
The State required that it escape detection.
We damped our nascent love and I submitted
To serve the Lord to whom I was committed.
But marriage was a chain constricting me,
Only his death or mine could set me free.
I've no excuse, no fatal flaw to blame
As step by step to my dark fate I came
Thinking that peace and happiness would follow.
But human hearts reject such goals as hollow.
Our crimes committed, we have no recourse
To any joy, but only to remorse.
I now recall far happier times than this
When I felt all the joys of wedded bliss.
But I saw Claudius and seeing, fell
From Heaven's forecourt to the gates of Hell.
Claudius never strove to win a place
At court. His pride soon led to his disgrace.
I pitied him, and as my pity grew,
My husband turned offensive in my view.
I came to think that his unfeeling heart
Deserved some sort of vengeance on my part.
Whatever I desired then was permitted.
The King was to my care alone committed
And from my hands alone my Lord received
Those medicines upon which he relied
Were by my hands selected and supplied.
My evil partner's soul took charge of mine
And my weak hand fulfilled his foul design.
I went into my husband's room, concealing
The terror and the guilt that I was feeling.
But as I realized I'd never see
The King again, remorse swept over me.
Thus when a monstrous deed we would commit,
Nature arises and denounces it.
In vain I sought my boldness to regain,
My blood was ice, confusion in my brain,
Unable to confront my crime, I fled,
Leaving the fatal cup beside his bed.
But I had scarcely left his room behind

When his death agonies obsessed my mind.
Returning reason, hating my decision,
Inspired in me this horrifying vision.
Panicked, I tried to force myself to think
He had not yet consumed that fatal drink;
I hastily returned. Perhaps I planned
To dash the drink I'd left him from his hand,
Or maybe to atone for how I'd tried
To kill him, I'd fall lifeless by his side.
I entered, but the heavens, unforgiving,
Had sealed my doom. He was no longer living.
Remorse had come too weakly and too late.
The cruel gods now left me to my fate.

ELVIRE:          Oh, heavens!

GERTRUDE:                    I ran in terror from the sight
Avoiding others in my headlong flight.
Gaining at last my chambers—who can blame me?—
Remorse and grief together overcame me.
The sobs and cries you overheard were part
Of that consuming torment in my heart.
Confessing this is painful, but I know
That pain is only part of what I owe.
Alas, since making that accursed decision
That fatal goblet never leaves my vision.
What hope for happiness is there in view
When my dear son seems to be dying too?
First of my husband, then of son bereft,
The horror of my crime alone is left.
As punishment Nature has sent its dart
Into the deepest chambers of my heart.

ELVIRE:          Your son lives still; it is for you to find
The secret woes that so torment his mind.
Pursue that project; none will interfere.
I can't believe, since he still holds you dear,
That Claudius ...

GERTRUDE:                    That union I must shun.
Our wedding torches would blot out the sun.
Our souls, united by a deed so base
Would bring that holy knot into disgrace.

I seek no pleasures of the marriage bed,
Shame and reproach should be my lot instead.
I'd like to trumpet to the universe
My crime, and let it crush me with its curse.
To marry now would add more fire
Unto the gods' already raging ire.
I would their vengeance they'd no longer stay
But send me to my death this very day!
How just and fearful would be the impression
If my own son could punish my transgression!
How terrible but fitting it would be
If he'd avenge his father's death on me.
Unnatural, yes, but what defense have I?
Nature I was too eager to defy.
I did not hesitate its laws to spurn,
Why should my son not follow in his turn?

ELVIRE:     Leave these dark thoughts, Madam, consider how
To bear yourself. Norceste is coming now.

## Scene 2

### GERTRUDE, ELVIRE, NORCESTE

GERTRUDE (*going to* NORCESTE): My Lord, a grieving mother begs your aid.
My son grows weak, near death I am afraid.
Try to find out from what this woe has grown.
I put my trust in you, and you alone.
To us his heart is closed and locked but we
Hope that your friendship may provide the key.
I'll leave you with him, tell me what you learn,
His mental health in everyone's concern.
We trust in you, Sir, Hamlet and the state
And I as well, you see the stakes are great.

## Scene 3

### NORCESTE

NORCESTE:     What frightful hidden woe can Hamlet bear
That his own loving mother cannot share?

News of his father's death caused such concern
In me, at once I felt I must return.
Denmark's a land where plots are always rife
Susceptible to rapid change and strife.
But Hamlet has no enemies who wait
To take advantage of his troubled state.
His heart is virtuous, his motives pure.
Of Claudius and the Queen I'm not so sure.
Suspicion at the court is always wise,
Great secrets often greater crimes disguise.


## Scene 4

### NORCESTE, VOLTIMAND

VOLTIMAND (*upstage*): Advance no more, my Lord, the Prince is mad.
A more distracted day he's never had!
His fearful cries resound throughout the palace
As if a vengeful god in ruthless malice
Were punishing him for some frightful act.
Tonight his terrors once again attacked
Dark shadows drove him shrieking to my arms,
Again the prey to unrevealed alarms.
And yet despite his suffering and his fear,
He still can sense it when a friend is near.

NORCESTE:     Permit me, then ...


## Scene 5

### HAMLET, VOLTIMAND, NORCESTE

HAMLET:                          Flee, fearful apparition
Back to your tomb! Forsake your cursed mission!

VOLTIMAND:     You hear?

HAMLET:                          Look up! You see that thing of hell,
Above my head and at my heels as well.
He comes to me with death.

VOLTIMAND:                            Prince, calm your fear.
Open your eyes. Your friend, Norceste, is here.
His tender friendship brought him home again.

HAMLET:          Dear friend! Your face alleviates my pain.
Companion of my childhood! What delight!
My tortured heart grow tranquil in your sight.
That heart, so long tormented, finds a balm
In your return, and once again grows calm.
How glad I am, my friend, to see you here.

NORCESTE:       My Prince, take heart, and put aside your fear.
You're much too young to give way to the folly
Of being overcome by melancholy.
When sad events befall us it is just
That we feel sadness. Surely, Prince we must.
Still we must set some limits to our woe.

HAMLET:          You've been abroad in England. Do you know
What I have suffered?

NORCESTE:                           Yes.

HAMLET:                                        My father dead,
I'd rather have the sun eclipsed instead.

NORCESTE:       Surely in time Nature will work her cure.
Send consolation ...

HAMLET:                                  Never, I am sure.
Remember, friend, with what a tender gaze
My father oversaw my childhood days.
I never thought Fate so coldly might
Break in and take him from my loving sight.
He is no more and now, among the shades
He disappears, his memory quickly fades.
His deeds and death now scarcely merit mention
As courtly pleasures clamor for attention.
While I alone, eyes turned down toward the sod,
Seek traces of the paths my father trod.
But you are welcome back and I must learn
What brought about your unforeseen return.
When you said England lost, without a warning

Its king, plunging its people into mourning.
My father dead, and all my senses reeling,
I thought I understood what you were feeling.
But I assumed you surely would remain
Abroad and shun this pitiful domain.

NORCESTE:    Scarcely had I dispatched the information
To you about the King's assassination,
And how the British people, horrified
At hearing how their royal master died,
Demanded that the secrets be revealed
That in those castle walls were still concealed,
When my report to you was overtaken
By news from Denmark, that it had been shaken
As well by royal death. Then with all speed
I hurried here to help you in your need.
To wipe away your tears, to share your grief
And offer what I can to bring relief.
I knew your loss would deeply have affected
Your spirits, but I wouldn't have expected
This mortal pallor, this extreme disgust
At everything, this lassitude. You must
Subdue your passion, give to reason heed,
Accept whatever sorrow the gods decreed.
My friend, I scarcely can believe that you
Are the same Hamlet that I one time knew.
Dear Prince, tell me what secrets you are keeping
That justify such agonies, such weeping.

HAMLET:    Alas! When I received the news you sent
Of England's foul and treacherous event.
It was as if this clarified my sight
With dazzling but terrifying light.
I realized the horror that befell
The English king might fit our case as well.
My father's death I saw with opened eyes;
In sleepless nights I heard his dying cries
And saw him reappear as if demanding
I view his death with better understanding.

NORCESTE:    Don't be mislead ... a random parallel ...

HAMLET:    The end's the same, why not the cause as well?
Believe me, friend, I have firm ground to think
My father perished from a poisoned drink.
Heaven and Hell join in this accusation
And urge revenge for his assassination.
In bloody letters on the walls I read
Heaven's command to carry out this deed.

NORCESTE:    Have these mysterious orders caused the pain
And trouble you are suffering? Explain
This further.

HAMLET:                        Don't assume my disposition
Arises from unfounded supposition.
My father twice has come to me in dreams
Not wrathful, not belligerent, he seems
Morose and mournful, and his eyes o'erflow
With tears expressive of the deepest woe.
I tried to speak to him, consumed with fear
To see so ominous a form appear.
What was his fate, I asked. Could he confide
What we could look for on the other side.
Were there eternal torments that awaited
Us there, or could our sins be expiated?
"My son," he said, "such questions are forbidden.
Such secrets from all mortals must be hidden.
But one dark fact I will not try to hide;
Kings suffer greatly on the other side.
If Heaven open discourse would allow,
Your face would grow more pale than mine is now.
To grasp the crown your hands would hesitate
If you could really know its fearful weight.
This weight is scarcely felt in earthly realms
But in the tomb its burden overwhelms."

NORCESTE:    Great gods!

HAMLET:                        Tell me, spirit both dark and dear,
Why you have left death's realm and journeyed here?
Why do you seek me out when soon I too
Will end this troubled life and be with you.
Keep closed those frozen lips, do not reveal
Death's secrets you're commanded to conceal.

Trembling then I ask, what do you seek
From me? I charge you, fearful phantom, speak!
"My son, I bring a task for you," he said.
To bring my ashes peace, blood must be shed.
It's said I died of illness. This report
Is but a lie to pacify the court.
Your mother, yes my most perfidious wife
Prepared the drink that robbed me of my life.
Love for that villain Claudius drove her to it.
He was the one who spurred her on to do it."
With this, he disappeared.

NORCESTE:                                    Prince, what a toll
This must have taken on your troubled soul!

HAMLET:        Indeed, but don't believe that I accepted
At once this story, rather I suspected
Some test a cruel Heaven might devise
To denigrate my mother in my eyes,
And so by devious means sought to evade
The clear commandment that the ghost had made.
But all in vain, his spirit soon returned.
"My son," he cried. "Why it is you have spurned
My clear command? Arise now! Sleep no longer!
Revenge my death! No motive could be stronger.
The time for weeping on my urn is past.
Take up your sword, and seek revenge at last.
Take from the tomb my ashes, let them be
Grim witness of the evil done to me."
His cries awakened me, Norceste, I lept
From off my bed. Since then I have not slept
That dreadful shade now will not quit my thought.
I wonder through these castle halls distraught,
Pale, trembling, wretched, with no hope supplied,
That fearful spirit always by my side.
The dreadful story that the ghost imparted
Has left me terror-struck and broken-hearted.

NORCESTE:      The news I sent you from abroad, it seems
To me has conjured up these frightening dreams.
The English king was murdered, that is true,
But must his tragic fate apply to you?
The more you brood upon these thoughts by day,

The more within your dreams they will hold sway.
Your mind is troubled, and a willing host
To these disturbing visions, to this ghost.
To turn against your mother and this lord
Driven by fantasies, to draw your sword ...

HAMLET:         Ah, that's the fear that holds my arm in check.
I do not wholly trust what I suspect.
Murder revolts me, pity holds me back.
I would kill Claudius, a villain black,
But that would plunge a dagger in the breast
Of fair Ophelia, whom I love the best.
Whatever course I take, Norceste, I fear
I must do harm to someone I hold dear.
My mother I seem to see before me kneeling
Trying to quench the anger I am feeling.
"Hamlet," she says, "in pity sheathe your knife!
Forgive and spare the one who gave you life!
The breast that suckled you, the thighs that bore ..."
Can I maintain the rage I felt before?
O heavens, can it be that you demand
Such justice by my weak and mortal hand?
It is inhuman, choose some other course
Or someone I can slay without remorse.
To kill a villain is a small affair,
But even a guilty mother I must spare.

NORCESTE:       How has this palace managed to regain
Its joy so fast, while you endure such pain?

HAMLET:         Alas, the court almost at once returned
To normal life. His body quickly burned;
The ashes put within an urn and carried
Away so quick, I scarce knew he was buried.
Ye gods, if I could ...

NORCESTE:                              Speak, my lord, reveal
What could your troubled spirits calm and heal?
Whatever I can do for you I'll try.

HAMLET:         Not far from here my father's ashes lie.
A vulgar urn, no monument beside it
Almost unmarked, so well they sought to hide it.

Now I'm determined, we'll remove that urn,
Leave its dark recess empty and return
With it to some more open, public place
Reminding all who pass of our disgrace.
And my reward of all may be the best,
To clasp my father's ashes to my breast!

NORCESTE:     I'll do your bidding.

HAMLET:                                    One more thing to do.
We must seek out the Queen and Claudius too.
Report to them the English king's demise
And see if we can catch them by surprise.
See if by their reactions we can read
If my suspicions have some ground indeed.
Say that adultery, ambition, greed
Have caused the English monarchy to bleed.
If they but blanch at this, I'll know my course
And can pursue revenge without remorse.
Their darkest secrets brought into the sun,
We then can do whatever must be done.
Great gods, forgive the slow course I have taken
But in such things, I cannot be mistaken.
Such horror fills my heart at what you plan,
I must ask every question that I can.
Send me clear signs from sources I can trust
Assuring me that my revenge is just.
Upon their guilty faces let me read
The proofs of evil-doing that I need.

# ACT III

## Scene 1

### CLAUDIUS, POLONIUS

POLONIUS:    My Lord, your planning all has been in vain.
Hamlet is to be crowned, the fact is plain.
What can we do, the Queen herself has stated
That her  weak son would be so elevated.
Your projects lie in ruins, nothing left,
You are of friends and hope alike bereft.

CLAUDIUS:    I won't attend the crowning, and endeavor
To put it off for now, perhaps forever.
The Queen, it's clear, seeks to consolidate
Her son's control and power in the state.
But when some counterplot we have devised,
Our own part in it we must keep disguised.
With utmost prudence and by indirection
We must proceed, to keep us from detection.
Take this occasion to survey the court.
Find out where we can garner more support.
The soldiers and their captains are secured;
Their loyalty by gifts of gold insured.
My friends will not desert me, even they
Most prone to waver, bribery will sway.
The bounteous booty we shall all divide
Will quite suffice to keep them on my side.
We'll treat the State as would a ravenous beast
And they like predators, will share the feast.
Their hearts, their arms, their consciences are mine.
They now await for me to give the sign.

POLONIUS:    But if the court awakens to your plot,
You have the nobles and the army, not
The people with you.

CLAUDIUS:                          Yes I have. My spies
Have been at work among them, spreading lies
Of how the Prince, driven by his desire
For power, murdered his own sire
By poisoned drink, placing himself at odds

With Nature's law, and the avenging gods.
His strange behavior, they assert, reveals
The guilt and self-abasement that he feels.
Bombarded by these oft-repeated lies,
The common folk are coming to despise
The Prince. It seems the people have a thirst,
Concerning their betters, to believe the worst.

POLONIIUS:    But watch Norceste, scarcely had he arrived
When all of Hamlet's following revived.
Emboldened now, they gather and they plan
And will upset your wishes if they can.
But I am well aware of what they're doing.

CLAUDIUS:    Tell me at once if you sense trouble brewing.
Give these developments your close attention
As we prepare the way for my ascension.
But Hamlet and the Queen are coming now.


## Scene 2

### CLAUDIUS, POLONIUS, HAMLET, GERTRUDE

GERTRUDE:    Why these tears, Hamlet, why this furrowed brow?
Command those clouds around you to depart
And let your mother's voice lift up your heart.
Consider, when these shadows are defeated,
That glorious throne upon which you'll be seated.
All join with me in wishing you the best,
The noble Claudius, the good Norceste,
To these I add my love and my support.
A brilliant day is dawning for our court.
The people clamor for you to appear
And launch into your glorious career.
You seem to them a rising star, whose light
Will soon dispel the terrors of the night.
You do not answer. Why do you continue
To hide from me those mysteries within you?
Give me a single word. My fear has grown ...

CLAUDIUS:    Let Hamlet be. His secrets are his own.
Hamlet, your mother knows, and I have said it,

Your sorrow for your father does you credit.
The tears you've shed for him were much deserved,
But mourning's expectations have been served.
As time goes on reasonable man
Takes heart and carries on as best he can.
Your friend Norceste's return gives indication
That Heaven seeks to send you consolation.
Friendship provides a barrier to grief.

HAMLET:      It's true, his presence brings me some relief.
Have you seen him?

CLAUDIUS:                              Not yet. He clearly sought
To seek you first.

HAMLET:                        Perhaps, and yet he ought
To tell you of the King of England's fate.

CLAUDIUS:      Rumors abound. The mystery is great.

HAMLET:      Is it known by whose hand ...

NORCESTE:                                When a king dies,
All sort of talk about the palace flies,
Some based on fact, some totally absurd.
Distinguishing is hard, thus, I have heard
Some talk of poison, surely an invention.

CLAUDIUS:      Could anyone at court have that intention?

HAMLET:      Who is suspected of so foul a crime?

NORCESTE:      One highly honored in a happier time.

HAMLET:      His name?

NORCESTE:                        A prince of loftiest position,
Whom one would think to be above suspicion.

GERTRUDE:      Were others named, or did he act alone?

NORCESTE:      One more ...

HAMLET:                    The Queen ...

GERTRUDE:                                  O heavens, is that known
                    For certain ...

NORCESTE:                    I'm not sure.

GERTRUDE:                                        But there must be
                    Some motive given for such infamy.

NORCESTE:      Adulterous lust, and royal power taken.
                    (*aside to* HAMLET)
                    He trembles not.

HAMLET:         (*aside to* NORCESTE) No, but the Queen is shaken!

CLAUDIUS:       Ambition, love, intrigue, these are the sort
                    Of rumor that bedevil every court.
                    But Prince, let's leave such images alone.
                    Let foreign shores pursue them on their own.
                    We have our own misfortunes, let's not borrow
                    Another kingdom's misery and sorrow.
                    England has often been the home of crimes.

HAMLET:         As other lands have been in other times.
                    Let's go, Norceste.

## Scene 3

### CLAUDIUS, GERTRUDE

GERTRUDE:                    What think you?

CLAUDIUS                                        I am sure
                    He suspects nothing.

GERTRUDE:                                  Would my soul were pure.

CLAUDIUS:       Your fears are groundless.

## Scene 5

### GERTRUDE *alone.*

GERTRUDE:                                 Why do I have these fears?
Claudius dares, while I dissolve in tears.
Where can I find asylum and relief?
Can I look to my son to ease my grief?
Nature I'm certain would advise me so.
I cannot trust in Claudius, I know.
Misgivings rack my troubled soul. I tremble
With secret horror. How can I dissemble?
But who is here? Ophelia!

## Scene 6

### GERTRUDE, OPHELIA

OPHELIA:                                 Madame, please!
I must confess before you on my knees!

GERTRUDE:     What's this?

OPHELIA:                                 Alas, I know that you have sought
The secret making Hamlet so distraught.

GERTRUDE:     You know it?

OPHELIA:                                 First, you must give me your word
You will forgive me all, once you have heard.

GERTRUDE:     What awful crime, Ophelia, have you done?
Is Claudius ... but tell me of my son.
Have you found out his secret? Then impart
It to his mother. Heal her aching heart.

OPHELIA:     Madam ...

GERTRUDE:                                 Please tell me. I will understand.

OPHELIA:     You will recall the late King's firm command
That Hamlet and myself should separate,

GERTRUDE:                                                   Will he not surmise
Our guilt from the expressions in our eyes?
How I have suffered, trying to keep still.

CLAUDIUS:     Fear only your own heart and trust your will.
Let them talk on. Be sure you don't betray
Uneasiness at anything they say.
Always dissimulate; make it your goal
To keep your feelings under your control.
Still, I will carefully pursue this matter.
Hamlet's report may be but idle chatter.
But if he has some secret we must find it;
His idle talk may have some aim behind it.
We seem secure, but wise men are aware
That hidden dangers may lurk anywhere.


## Scene 4

### CLAUDIUS, GERTRUDE, POLONIUS

POLONIUS:     Madam, all's ready. It is you alone
Who must decide when Hamlet takes the throne.
The people are prepared for his ascension
As are the nobles. It's their firm intention
To put the fate of Denmark in his hands
And welcome him as ruler of these lands.
But, Prince, it would be well if you'd appear
And calm the troubled spirits. There is fear
Of war and Hamlet's health. Norceste's return
Contributed as well to this concern.
But show yourself and you will dissipate
These clouds, restoring order to the State.

CLAUDIUS:     I will respond as once to what you ask.
Prudence and duty call me to this task.
You, Madam, seek your son out. Try to find
What secret troubles occupy his mind.
A virtuous son should be at ease confiding
Unto his mother everything he's hiding.
Mingle your tears with his, share in his woes
And see what he is willing to disclose.
Come, let us go.

Never attempting to communicate.
Hamlet convinced me to defy this ban.

GERTRUDE:      What?

OPHELIA:                  Into hopeless love we fell. I can
Confess it now. Our love had to be hidden,
Locked in our hearts, because it was forbidden.
I was the weaker, Hamlet was the stronger,
At last I could restrain myself no longer;
I dared to speak and he reciprocated,
But once expressed, his love degenerated
Into his present state, which so alarms you.
This is the way that thwarted passion harms you.
My share in this at last I have confessed.
Punish my crime however you think best.
Even the pain of death could be endured
If by my death Prince Hamlet might be cured.

GERTRUDE:      No! Live, love, and be happy. Your confessing
I see not as an evil, but a blessing.
At last I see into Prince Hamlet's soul.
Our heart is never under our control.
I understand the suffering you've known,
Loving, but forced to feel that love alone.
Now, finally, you two can live as one;
I've but to say the word and it is done.
Reign with my son, when you pronounce your vows,
I'll place myself the crown upon your brows.
I'll take to Claudius this joyful news
And I am sure that he will share my views.
How quickly Hamlet's sorrows will dissipate
When fair Ophelia has become his mate!
Embrace me, daughter. Celebrate this day
When love and virtue have regained their sway.

ACT IV

Scene 1

HAMLET

HAMLET:    So far I've worked in vain. The trap I laid
To catch him out, he managed to evade.
My guilty mother also did not fail
In her compsure, though her cheek grew pale.
Can this vile Claudius have such self-control
That crime like his weighs not upon his soul?
Any remorse he feels he does not show.
He seems as pure as the new-fallen snow.
Could they be innocent? Oh, troubling thought!
My father's ghost insists that they are not!
But could that spirit too be an illusion,
Born out of my despair and my confusion?
If I have been mistaken, or misled
A mother's guiltless blood will I have shed ...
I cannot choose, not action brings release
And as I hesitate, my doubts increase.
Life is a weight too heavy to endure.
Perhaps then death provides me with a cure.
There suffering mortals finally can cast
Aside their troubles, and find peace at last.
To die! Fear ceases when we cease to be
To sleep, perhaps to dream eternally.
Perhaps ... that cold word makes us hesitate
As at the very door of death we wait.
We cannot leap into that vast abyss
And stumble back from that world into this.
However great our troubles, still we fear
That unknown country may be worse than here.
Our terror of the unknown is so great,
We hesitate to enter death's dark gate.
How many otherwise would cast aside
The burdens that they bear and rush inside!
How tempting is death's ever-open portal
To every weak and tempest-battered mortal!
His troubles weigh him down, but even so
He fears worse troubles that he does not know.
Forbidding future, you inspire my fear

But through my anguish, I will perservere.
But here's Ophelia. Would that her gentleness
Could sooth my pain!

OPHELIA:                              Hamlet, I must confess
I've told the Queen that your infirmity
Has risen from your father's stern decree.
Her love for you spurs her to see you cured
Of those cruel sufferings you have endured.
Learning the cause was love, she eagerly
Expressed her heartfelt wish to set you free.
I only wish you could have shared the sight
Of her relief and her unfeigned delight!
Our love is such a joy to her, she said,
She'll place our crowns herself upon our head.
But why receive such happy news with sighs?
What troubles seem reflected in your eyes?
Happiness is at hand! Do you not care?

HAMLET:     Our joy is further off than you're aware.

OPHELIA:     What are you saying? Prince, your words suggest
You still feel suffering within your breast.
Your love for me perhaps begins to pall.

HAMLET:     Ophelia, you don't understand at all.
My heart, so long committed to your favors,
Remains so still, my passion never wavers;
Unto the tomb this passion I will keep.

OPHELIA:     Why then, my Lord, do you not cease to weep?
Why are you still unable to disguise
The dark despair reflected in your eyes?
What bitter poison do you still consume?

HAMLET:     Seek not to taste it; it would be your doom.

OPHELIA:     The wedding bonds that would join you to me
In happy union, then are not to be.
It was an idle dream that now must die.

HAMLET:     My love was real; the rest was all a lie.

OPHELIA:     Cruel Prince. Your heart is closed to me for good?

HAMLET:      Alas, I would unlock it if I could!
             An obstacle of which you're unaware
             Opposes us and dooms me to despair.
             I suffer for the state in which I've kept you,
             But I would die before I could accept you.
             If fate had willed, the earth would never see
             A pair united in such bliss as we.
             Our wishes and our hearts in sweet communion,
             Heaven would rain blessings on our union.
             But I will speak no more of that lost bliss.
             Your heart loves mine, I'm quite aware of this
             And yet ... oh misery!

OPHELIA:                         Go on!

HAMLET:                                Not I!

OPHELIA:     Why not?

HAMLET:                     Our choice is but to die.

OPHELIA:     You want to die?

HAMLET:                         It's time that I was gone.
             Despair of love and life too drives me on.
             Days of pure pleasure and of joy serene
             On this accursed earth are rarely seen.
             Sorrows instead plague us with constant pain.
             Pleasures are brief, while sufferings remain!
             How can we best respond to this condition?
             Regard whatever happens with suspicion.
             Hear what men say, but don't believe a word.
             Consider all their quarrels as absurd.
             Trust not in friendship, knowing well that rarely
             You'll find a person who will treat you fairly.
             The truth, so noble even kings should use it
             Instead finds only people who abuse it.
             Wars and betrayals, projects gone awry;
             Honors accorded none can justify.
             Everywhere plots and plotting, casual hates,
             And poison fed to unsuspecting mates.

Since Heaven pours these ills upon my head,
It certainly must want to see me dead.
What care the gods who witness my distress
If I live on a moment more or less.
Languishing, beaten, wracked with every breath
My living is what pains me, not my death.

OPHELIA:    Heavens! What demon holds you in its grasp?
And has he made you barbarous at last?
I've dreamed to calm my lover's heart one day
And his abundant tears to wipe away.
Our marriage, I imagined, would give life
New pleasures and new duties, as his wife.
No longer speaking of myself alone,
Has your own life no value of its own?
Heir to the throne, have you no obligation
To listen to those cries arising from your nation:
"Our liberty, our fate is in your hands.
Are we not bound by patriotic bands?
In your strong arm we trust for our defense.
Strike down oppressors, save the innocents.
Protect your subjects, strong compassion show them
These are the sacred duties that you owe them."

HAMLET:    Alas!

OPHELIA:              Fear not, but reign!

HAMLET:                              What do you ask?
If only I were equal to that task!
You gods, you know, I wanted to create
A happy people in a prosperous State.
But you decided that I was unfit
To so aspire, and punish me for it.
(*to* OPHELIA): And you whom I offend though I adore
Renounce the hope to ever see me more.
Adieu ... I go ...

OPHELIA:                    I feel your sadness, yet
I also sense your suffering heart is set
Upon some secret woe ...

HAMLET:                    I?

OPHELIA:                                              You know I feel it.
                    Confide in me.

HAMLET:                           No, I cannot reveal it.

OPHELIA:        I know you're suffering. I could help you bear
                Your burdens, if you would but share.

HAMLET:         Their weight would crush you.

OPHELIA                                        Do not be so proud.
                Is weeping for you all I am allowed?
                To save you Hamlet, I would gladly die.
                Witness that death; you'll find I do not lie.

HAMLET:         Unhappy woman! Do you want to share
                Those cries of vengeance I hear in the air?
                Do you desire to see dead spirits rise
                And manifest themselves before your eyes?
                By day, wish you dark shadows in your sight
                Replaced with threatening fiery forms at night?
                Hell's torments seek to hold your spirit fast
                And freeze your heart's blood in an icy blast!

OPHELIA:        You terrify me, yet you must reveal
                The secret of this suffering you feel.

HAMLET:         I only wish to die.

OPHELIA:                                    I don't believe you.

HAMLET:         Tremble.

OPHELIA:            I fear not.

HAMLET:                                Fly.

OPHELIA:                                    I will not leave you.

## Scene 2

### HAMLET, GERTRUDE, OPHELIA

OPHELIA (*to* GERTRUDE *entering*):
   Ah, Madam! Speak to Hamlet. Take my part!
   I'm powerless, it seems, to touch his heart.
   Draw out his secret, Nature I suspect
   Is stronger still than love in its effect.

GERTRUDE:  Hamlet, do you still turn aside and frown?
   Do you still wander with your eyes cast down?
   Do fear-provoking objects yet surround you?
   I left you suffering, so have I found you?
   With all your courage can you not be led
   To think that better days may lie ahead?
   Mournful or happy, all of us must die.

HAMLET:  Madame, I know it.

GERTRUDE:        Why then choose to sigh?
   Why waste away your days in secret sorrow?
   Life for the day, leave mourning for tomorrow.
   Whatever your concerns, you should confide them.

HAMLET:  They are so ill, that it is best to hide them.

GERTRUDE:  Is there some crime of which you are ashamed?

HAMLET:  I have done nothing for which to be blamed.

GERTRUDE:  If that is so, how can confession hurt you?
   Your downcast air does not sit well with virtue.
   Consider the appearance you project.

HAMLET:  My heart is pure. What have I to protect?

GERTRUDE:  Why then this silence, if there's no guilt in it?
   My worries and my fears grow by the minute.
   I beg you by the love you have received
   From the first moment when you were conceived,
   Confide in me ... but no, I see you frozen
   Within the prison you yourself have chosen.

Why can you neither speak nor take to flight?
Some fearful vision seems within your sight.


HAMLET (*seeing his father's ghost*): Do you not see him. Look, I see him pass!
What do you want?

GERTRUDE:                                          To see you cured, alas!

HAMLET (*still observing the ghost*):
Look, it is he! He threatens! He advances!
Where can I hide, where flee his horrid glances?
I'm lost!

GERTRUDE:              My son!

HAMLET:                                I can't do what you ask ...

GERTRUDE:      What's that?

HAMLET:                                Impossible. So foul a task
A caring Heaven never would impose.
Can I believe, dark spirit, you arose
To bring me messages so much at odds
With what should be the will of righteous gods!
Unless you're sent from Hell, what is the cause
That puts you so at odds with Nature's laws?
But if it's Heaven's orders you fulfill,
Give me the strength to carry out its will.

GERTRUDE:      What will, my son?

HAMLET:                                You think that the confusion
In which I'm plunged is merely an illusion.

GERTRUDE:      How can you doubt it? Reason has forsaken
Your troubled mind...

HAMLET                                Madame, you are mistaken.

It's all too real.

GERTRUDE:                    Some secret struggles tear

Your soul apart, and leave but chaos there!

HAMLET (*to his mother*): It's you who these destructive passions bred!
(*to* OPHELIA): And do you know for whom your tears are shed?


### Scene 3

### CLAUDIUS, GERTRUDE, HAMLET, OPHELIA

HAMLET (*continuing*): Heavens! It's Claudius!

GERTRUDE:                                         Sir, what brings you here?
Was it to see my son, whose death is near ...

CLAUDIUS:    I thought their nuptials you were arranging.

GERTRUDE:    So I desired, but find my son unchanging.
He is determined he is going to die
Without to anyone confiding why.

CLAUDIUS:    I am astonished at a will so steeled
That even to love's arrows he will not yield.
He clearly feels he cannot disobey
The bar his father put across his way.
Madam, you can revoke that harsh decree.
I will choose Hamlet if you set him free.
A modest wedding ...

HAMLET (*suddenly arousing himself, as if awakening*): You will post no bans!
Abandon, rebel, your audacious plans.
I am your king, to me you must defer.
Ophelia belongs to me and I to her.
No other mortal dares to wish her hand.
My will is sovereign, as you understand.
This heart, that you thought weak and void of power
Has not, you see, yet reached its final hour.
(*looking at* Claudius)
Doubtless some here are jealous of my throne.
But though my death be near, let it be known
I will not leave 'til I have carried through
(*to* CLAUDIUS) The task that Heaven has given me to do.

## Scene 4

### CLAUDIUIS, GERTRUDE, OPHELIA

CLAUDIUS:     Madam, what could this sudden outburst mean?
GERTRUDE:     Whatever he says, I will not intervene.
              (*to* OPHELIA) Come with me. Follow Hamlet. We must try
              To save him, or if all else fails, to die.

## Scene 5

### CLAUDIUS

CLAUDIUS:     What unknown trouble permeates this palace?
              Whence comes Prince Hamlet's sudden rage and malice?
              Does he suspect my plots? Could he have guessed
              His father's murder was at my behest?
              Here is Polonius.

## Scene 6

### CLAUDIUS, POLONIUS

CLAUDIUS:                         The Prince has broken
              His silence. Now I wish he had not spoken.
              He just now left. There isn't any doubt
              His once internal rage has broken out.
              Whatever he knows or guesses, I can see
              His filial rage is focusing on me.
              But while such undirected rage he sows,
              I will find openings to direct my blows.
              I will not wait until he grows in power
              And casts me down, but I will seize my hour!
              If we delay much longer he will bind us!
              Will all our friends at court remain behind us?

POLONIUS:     They wait on you, and numerous is their tally.
              The shadow Prince only a few can rally.
              This very day can bring about your fate,

|                |                                                        |
|----------------|--------------------------------------------------------|
|                | But all may crumble if you hesitate.                   |
|                | Norceste among the people spreads alarms.              |
|                | To Hamlet's followers he is giving arms.               |
|                | We're at a fateful moment, in my view,                 |
|                | Fall upon them before they fall on you.                |
| CLAUDIUS:      | Ye gods! I am beset on every side.                     |
|                | I'm near the throne and yet the gap is wide.           |
|                | So lately calm, now my whole being's shaking.          |
|                | What risks I run, what chances I am taking!            |

POLONIUS:    Don't hesitate, while you have the capacity
To overcome all odds by your audacity.
But if you pause now, trying to arrange
Some better moment ...

CLAUDIUS:                              Everything may change!
Let's act! It's time.

POLONIUS:                              My Lord, I clearly see
This is the hour that gives us victory.
Your friends are all prepared. Don't hesitate,
Dare all. They'll follow you.

CLAUDIUS                              My soldiers wait.
The Council ...

POLONIUS:                    Also waits. A faithful guard
Protects the place. Your enemies are barred.

CLAUDIUS:    Let's join them then, and hope they understand
That everything must go as we have planned.
I'll start by saying that the Queen has shown
Most clearly she wants Hamlet on the throne.
Dissembling, then, I'll struggle to convince
The Council members to support the Prince.
Some will resist, arguing his condition
Makes him unfit for any such position.
His brooding state, his mental aberration
Would be an insult to the Danish nation.
Others will rise in his defense to speak,
Employing arguments diffuse and weak.
At length they'll come together in accord.
Hamlet they'll find unfit to be their Lord.

And then the Council, free to choose at last,
Will think of me and of my glorious past.
In arms so powerful, with heart so great,
They'll hail me as the ruler of the state
And I, astounded by this show of favor,
Will hesitate at first and seem to waver.
But finally to the torrent I will yield,
Pitying Hamlet and with joy concealed,
Accept with humbleness the heavy crown,
Appearing falsely modest and cast down.

POLONIUS:    When through the Council you've attained your goal,
And Denmark's throne is under your control,
What then becomes of Hamlet? You must fear
The people, who, remember, hold him dear.
They might revolt.

CLAUDIUS:                  Then they will be defeated;
The Council gained; my plans are all completed.
The nobles and the army at my back
Will shield me well from any such attack.
They will pronounce me King. This sudden blow
Will stun the crowd and lay rebellion low.
Within the palace, order I'll restore.
The foolish Queen's protests I will ignore.
Hamlet I'll seize and have him locked away
Where he will never see the light of day.

POLONIUS:    Aren't you afraid the violence of your aim
Might then or later fan rebellion's flame?
Menace will always hang about your court
And Hamlet possibly regain support.
If ever Fate to him should power give ...

CLAUDIUS:    A King deposed has never long to live.
If any in his name try to rebel,
He'll find his tomb is not far from his cell.
All this my daughter never must discover.
She'd sacrifice her father for her lover.
The Council's gathering. Come follow me
And see your friend changed into royalty.

## ACT V

### Scene 1

HAMLET, NORCESTE, *bearing the urn.*

NORCESTE:      Regard, my Lord, this gloomy urn contains
All of a hero's pitiful remains!
No longer need you hide away your grief.
Weep on this urn and give your soul relief.
But yet for Claudius keep your anger strong,
Our right we must pursue against his wrong.
A portion of the Council and the court
Are with him, and he hopes with their support
To seize the crown. Consider, Prince, the cost.
He would be master, and you would be lost.
Ophelia and the Queen are unaware;
In his devices, neither has a share.
He claims to serve you, only with the thought
Of winning them and others to his plot.
His love for you is treason in disguise
Claimed only to divert suspicious eyes.
It's critical that we expose his feigning.
You still have loyal subjects, Prince, remaining.
I'll rush to gather them, those spirits true.
They're ready, as am I, to die for you.

HAMLET:       What do I care for glory or for throne?
Revenge I seek, that is my goal alone.

NORCESTE *leaves.*

### Scene 2

OPHELIA, HAMLET

OPHELIA:      My Lord, for one last time I humbly pray
You to attend to what I have to say.
The hatred toward my father than you bear
Has plunged my loving heart into despair.
He truly wishes us to be united.

He loves and pities you. He'd be delighted
To be your father, and make smooth your path.

HAMLET:      That monster!

OPHELIA:                              I'm appalled to see what wrath
Just naming him arouses in your heart.
What has he done to set you two apart?
Could it be he ... alas ...

HAMLET:                              What are you saying?

OPHELIA:      I know your sadness comes from vengeance weighing
Upon your heart. Though I had not suspected
Toward whom this secret anger was directed.
But now I see. My Lord, your hesitation
Suggests a victim of the highest station.
Dissemble then no longer. I've no doubt
Whom for your vengeance you have singled out.

HAMLET:      Go on.

OPHELIA:              It's my own father, I surmise.
When he came in now, your extreme surprise,
Your horror, your dark brow, your shortened breath,
Your whole demeanor seemed infused with death.
I have no doubt now. Your impulsive rage
Only the blood of Claudius can assuage.
But why this hatred? What is your design?
Why slay my father?

HAMLET:                              He, alas, slew mine.

OPHELIA:      You are mistaken!

HAMLET:                              No, my task is clear
From Heaven itself.

OPHELIA:                              Your fame will disappear!

HAMLET:      Except my fame as son.

OPHELIA:                              Then I as daughter
Must sacrifice my love to stop this slaughter.
I can't accept his guilt, and never will.
He is incapable of doing ill.
But even if my own eyes saw him do
Some deed considered criminal by you.
He is my father. I would still protect him.
Upon what grounds, in fact, do you suspect him?
I've seen the deep disturbance in your reason,
Your mind perturbed with murder and with treason.
Prey to such fancies, should you not be wary?
The crimes you find may be imaginary.
With blood so dear to me you would have reddened
Your hands? Is your humanity so deadened?
Alas, how deeply Heaven has misled me.
My hopeful heart assumed that you would wed me.
A happy marriage could we have enjoyed
But your illusions have such hopes destroyed.
There still is time, although I must accuse you
I love you still. My heart would not abuse you.
Upon my knees I beg you to forgive
The one who brought me life, and let him live.
If of some fearful crime he is the source,
Let vengeance take the form of long remorse.
Don't place between you this eternal wall
And cause the awful punishment to fall
On me, to quench the flame of love I've known
And to betray the blood that is my own.

HAMLET:       Alas, upon the scales you will have weighed
My love against the charge the gods have made.
Those fearful gods and powerful demand
Their vengeance be appeased with mortal hand.
In vain I tried to flee this fatal path
Before their altars I abjured my wrath.
A frightful voice pushed all my pleas aside:
"Have you avenged your father's death?" it cried.
I draw this dagger, but then love restrains,
Heaven insists and my despair remains.
Vengeance is called for when a father dies;
This sacred duty brooks no compromise.
Our love we can extinguish, but I never
Can raise my father. He is gone forever.

Blood has its claims. One can recover
From loss of dearest friend, or wife, or lover,
But only once do Heaven's gods provide us
A virtuous father, to preserve and guide us.

OPHELIA:        Yet listen, Hamlet ...

HAMLET:                          Weeping is in vain.
I see your love, your beauty, and your pain;
But if I let my love my anger subjugate,
And take you at the altar as my mate
At that same altar anger would inspire
Me once again to vengeance for my sire.
Love's claims are passing, Nature's claim endures.
My own blood's claims demand that I shed yours.
(*He sits.*)

OPHELIA:        You make me tremble. Are you judge and jury?
Are you unable to restrain this fury?
You see how our two duties intertwine.
You must avenge your father, I save mine.
I won't desert him. Knowing of your plan
I go to warm him, help him if I can,
Support him if I may to my last breath,
And if he perishes, join with him in death.
I can't believe your anger has such might
That you'd view such destruction with delight.
I hope that time and love will change your view,
But if your error you cannot subdue,
I'll no more dream of joining you as wife
But cast my lot with him who gave me life.


Scene 3

HAMLET

HAMLET:        I breathe again. Love's claims I cast aside
While those of blood and vengeance still abide.
(*regarding the urn*)
Source of my heartfelt vows, oh fearful urn
With tears and trembling to you I turn.
Yours is the power to strengthen and to shape me
Your foe, barbarous Claudius, won't escape me.
But even if avenged a hundred-fold,

You still are dead, your noble body cold.
My most unhappy father whom I mourn
Without release, why was I ever born?
You were deprived of even a final frown;
You never saw the hand that struck you down!
Cruel poisoner, there is but little time
For you to taste the fruits of your base crime.
Ere long my vengeance-seeking sword will rest
In your foul heart within your murderous breast.
These hands will slay you, cruel, perfidious one,
Here is the altar where your blood will run.
O Heaven, I seem to feel the ashes stirring
What miracle, my father, is occurring?
What moves you, what more goad would you supply me
Seek you to strengthen, or to terrify me?
I hear your murmur, pitiful remains,
My bloody sword will wash away your stains.
I live only to serve you, precious urn
And when that's done, I'll perish in my turn.
But who is here?


## Scene 4

### GERTRUDE, HAMLET

GERTRUDE:                         My son, why so severe
An aspect? Why a visage so austere?

HAMLET:      Mother ...

GERTRUDE:                         Explain yourself.

HAMLET:                                   Do not come near me.

GERTRUDE:      What's this?!

HAMLET:                         Then tremble! You have cause to fear me!

GERTRUDE:      What cause?

HAMLET:                         Can you not guess the sacrifice
Heaven demands as my redemption's price?

GERTRUDE:     Ye gods!

HAMLET:       Where is my father? Whose the hand
              That gave him poison? By whom was it planned?
GERTRUDE:     My son!

HAMLET:                    You thought that vengeance would remain
              Within his tomb, but all such thoughts were vain,
              She has emerged.

GERTRUDE:                              Oh gods!

HAMLET:                                    I've seen your mate.

GERTRUDE:              What does he want?

HAMLET:                                    Your blood ... to expiate.

GERTRUDE:     What! I commit a deed so heinous? No!

HAMLET:       Complain to Heaven then, which told me so.
              Your time has come.

GERTRUDE:                              You dare to think that I ...

HAMLET:       I would myself on my own dagger die
              Were I convinced that such a charge could start
              Within my troubled and suspicious heart,
              But it was Heaven who spoke, I merely heard.
              Twice from among the shades of death has stirred
              My father, to this fearful truth reveal.
              Beyond belief it seems, but all too real.
              Twice have the laws of death been set aside
              For him to state your guilt. Could he have lied?
              You think these charges from my fancy grew,
              But if the gods our murderers pursue
              If they rule all, then they can clearly choose
              To summon up the dead to voice their views.
              The power of Heaven far exceeds our ken.
              Its vengeance mocks the feeble wills of men.
              To point out murder signs they can provide;
              Statues can speak, and graves can open wide.
              The murderer discovers one he's slain

In order to condemn him, comes again.
Beside the light of truth the gods display
Pale grows the former glorious light of day.
Madam, you tremble.

GERTRUDE:                          Ah, how can I hear
Such horrors without giving way to fear?
Leave me, my son, my little strength is spent ...

HAMLET:     Why tremble if your heart is innocent?

GERTRUDE:     I tremble at the fury in your voice.

HAMLET:     Defend yourself then; offer me some choice.

GERTRUDE:     What must I do?

HAMLET:                   You must ... think of some way
To give me some belief in what you say.

GERTRUDE:     Speak on.

HAMLET (*presenting the urn to her*): Take up this urn and on it swear
Your total innocence in this affair.
Dare you?

GERTRUDE:                    Give it to me.

HAMLET:                      You hesitate?

GERTRUDE:     Forgive me. My disturbance is still great.

HAMLET :     Now swear ... (*putting the urn in her hands*):

GERTRUDE:     Yes ... yes ... upon this urn I swear ...
Ah no! All this is more than I can bear.
(*She falls unconscious into an armchair.* HAMLET *places
the urn on a table beside her.*)

HAMLET:     My mother!

GERTRUDE:                 I am dying!

HAMLET:                              Mother, please!
             Observe your son fall weeping at your knees!
             Heaven its grace for everyone has sent.
             Nothing is lost, if you will but repent.
             Let your offense be odious as it will,
             The goodness of the gods is greater still.
             Dear shade, at last you can depart in peace
             With these new sorrows can your sorrows cease.


### Scene 5

#### GERTRUDE, HAMLET, ELVIRE

ELVIRE:      Ah, tremble, Madam! Claudius's malice
             Has capped itself. He has besieged the palace!
             Norceste and others have secured the gates
             But cannot hold back Claudius and his mates.
             They're pushing forward, shortly we may face
             Bloody encounters in this very place.

HAMLET:      Claudius! (ELVIRE *leaves*.)


### Scene 6

#### GERTRUDE, HAMLET

GERTRUDE:                      My son!

HAMLET:                             The monster is at hand!
             Vengeance at last! Here will I take my stand.
             Heaven will guide the blows I give today.

GERTRUDE:    Pity, my son!

HAMLET:                       But none for him I slay!

GERTRUDE:    My son!

HAMLET (*The ghost appears*.): You see him there, that fearful shade?
                      He's come to see the debt of vengeance paid!

GERTRUDE:        What's this?

HAMLET (*speaking to the ghost*): I hear you; you must be obeyed!
                    (*to his mother*):
                    They both must bleed, he says ... why have you stayed?

GERTRUDE:        Great gods!

HAMLET:                                Do you not realize that you
                    Share in the guilt and must be punished too?

GERTRUDE (*falling in terror at* HAMLET's *feet*): Oh, Heaven!

HAMLET:                        Strike her? Your will be done!
                    You are my father ... but I am her son!

GERTRUDE:        My son!

HAMLET:            My mother! Ah my heart, abused,
                    By these conflicting passions is confused.
                    Fly from me or indeed I'll fly from you
                    In such a state I fear whatever I do.


                            Scene 7

            GERTRUDE, HAMLET, CLAUDIUS, POLONIUS, NORCESTE,
            VOLTIMAND, NOBLES, SOLDIERS, PEOPLE, *etc.*


NORCESTE (*entering, sword in hand*): People, save Hamlet.

CLAUDIUS:        Soldiers, hold him fast.

HAMLET:            Monster, your judgement faces you at last.
                    You see this urn?

CLAUDIUS:                        Well?

HAMLET:                            In its darkness lie
                    The ashes of the king you murdered!

CLAUDIUS:                                I?

HAMLET (*striking* CLAUDIUS, *and then addressing the assembly*):
          Yes, you, barbarian! And you, his friends,
          Follow him if you dare, and meet your ends!
          Let this expiring body serve as token
          That justice is restored; the gods have spoken.

VOLTIMAND *leaves with the body of* CLAUDIUS, *accompanied by* POLONIUS *and several other* CONSPIRATORS.

Scene 8

GERTRUDE, HAMLET, NORCESTE, NOBLES, etc.

HAMLET:          My vengeance is fulfilled by this dead lord,
          Back to your posts! Let order be restored.

NORCESTE:      Let Hamlet reign forever as our king.

HAMLET:          Now to the temple calming offerings bring.
          Heaven, that human crime will not forget
          Avenged my father!

GERTRUDE:                    No, alas, not yet.
          Claudius has suffered for his parricide,
          But still the gods remain unsatisfied.
          Another victim still must feed their wrath,
          Claudius led, but I trod in his path.
          No, I did more, I offered to my mate
          The fatal beverage that sealed his fate.
          His irritated ghost has been observed
          Urging my death, which I have well deserved.
          My generous son, his loving heart forgiving
          Refused this task, and so I am still living.
          Since he refused his father's stern command,
          It is for me to bow to that demand. (*She kills herself.*)

HAMLET:          Dear Mother, what cruel justice have you done?
          Forgiveness is possible.

GERTRUDE:                  Your vows, my son,
          Are cancelled now. Reign happy.

HAMLET:                                                    Mother, stay!
              Alas, forever she is torn away!


## Scene 9

### HAMLET, NORCESTE, NOBLES, *etc.*

HAMLET:        May the remorse and pardon of Heaven descend
               Upon you now and sanctify your end.
               This palace's dark walls have seen the pains
               Of many deaths, but virtue still remains.
               No longer death I seek, nor further strife
               As man and king, I'll seek fulfilling life.

*The curtain falls.*

# Romeo and Juliette

## 1772

# CAST OF CHARACTERS

FLAVIA

JULIETTE

ROMEO

CAPULET

ALBERIC

FERDINAND

MONTAGUE

AN OFFICER

SOLDIERS

COURTESANS

# ACT I

## Scene 1

### JULIETTE, FLAVIA

FLAVIA:      What, has your fearful heart again been stirred
             By some small passing rumor you have heard?
             Do you enjoy existing in alarm
             At minor matters that can do no harm?
             Why should it bother you if some old man
             Bored of his fading life conceives a plan
             To cross the Apennines and hide away
             In fair Verona, where he lives today?
             Think rather on Dolvedo, that brave knight
             Who gained such glory in the recent fight,
             Saving the life of young Duke Ferdinand
             Who covered him with honor for his stand.
             Proud Mantua, defeated in this fray
             Was forced to flee, and give to us the day.
             Our former enemies their forays cease
             Lay down their arms and sue to us for peace.
             Soon comes this hero, who so bravely fought
             His triumphs ought to occupy your thought.

JULIETTE:    Ah Flavia, 'tis not an easy part
             To love my hero with a tranquil heart.
             You know what obstacles must be endured
             Before our happy union is assured.
             Dolvedo, in my biased father's view,
             Is but a soldier and a parvenu.
             He little cares for military fame;
             He looks instead to blood and family name.
             He will acknowledge what the hero's done,
             But cannot bear to see him as a son,
             To enter an alliance of this sort
             To one without a family or support.

FLAVIA:      'Tis true, his past is hidden. No one knows
             The family from which Dolvedo arose.
             It seems the fate that raised him to such height
             Removed his humble origins from sight.

Ah, if the fame that now around him clusters
Would lend to some proud family new lustres,
If Heaven would grant unto a man so great
A famous name, a prosperous estate,
That would be just, but heaven did not deign
To do so ...

JULIETTE:                            And my hopes are thus in vain.
If only ...

FLAVIA:                    What?

JULIETTE:                         Do I dare to impart
To you the deepest secrets of my heart?

FLAVIA:    You may.

JULIETTE:           This Dolvedo, whom you know I adore
Whose prowess all Verona bows before ...

FLAVIA:    Yes?

JULIETTE:           He is Romeo.

FLAVIA:                          What?  Can it be?
No one could be of nobler birth than he!
Of virtuous Montague the eldest son,
The father rich in civic honors won,
A nobleman well known for his decision
To keep away from hatred and division,
Untouched by crime, from anger far apart
Loved by the town for his magnanimous heart,
Who more than twenty years has searched in vain
For a lost son, the source of endless pain.

JULIETTE:   In quiet seclusion, far from social snares
This noble father raised his virtuous heirs,
Until some brigands, in another's pay,
Sought twice to steal those precious sons away.
My uncle Roger sent them, to the shame
Of my dear father and my family's name.
Montague fought them, and his captured son
Out of their bloody grasp he briefly won,

His wounds nature allowed him to ignore
To save the son that he was fighting for.
But he grew weaker and could not prevent
The villains from achieving their intent.
After this bitter blow, the father never
Revived. He turned more hermit-like than ever.
He left our lands where he had felt such pain
And wanders with the sons that still remain.
His sons Renaud, Raymond, Dolce, Severe
Mourn with their father and his sorrows share.
Where they have gone nobody here has learned.
Yet Romeo, unrecognized, returned.
Escaped, but wandering, homeless, and in fear,
Father, in pity, gave him shelter here.
His heart, you know, is generous and mild;
He gladly sheltered this unhappy child.
And I within my heart began to feel
The budding love that time would soon reveal.
Interrogating him about his past,
I learned his true identity at last.
He knew his danger, I advised he take
A vulgar name for his own safety's sake.
Thus sheltered from his adversary's malice
Unknown he grew up with us in this palace.
The valiant Alberic and Theobald,
My brothers, him their other brother called.
The closest bonds of friendship there could be
Have long united Romeo with us three.
Matters went further, and I slowly found
We had become more and more closely bound.
It flattered me to have a power so great
Over his hopes, his prospects, and his fate.
I blessed that hidden place, where in disguise
My dear love hid away beneath my eyes.
Alas, I cried out, why has Heaven decided
To join our hearts whose houses are divided?
Perhaps its goodness lets us suffer now
But will in time support our love somehow.
Or turn that love to serve its own good ends
Making our feuding fathers faithful friends.
Mortals pursue their paths uncertainly
But Heaven guides them in their destiny.

FLAVIA:         But if (by some surprising twist of fate)
                This old man come to visit us of late
                Is Montague, fate surely will contrive
                To show him that his son is still alive.
                Romeo's scars will mark him as the one
                Thought dead, the long-ago abducted son.

JULIETTE:       What hope have we?

FLAVIA:                             Madame, do not despair.
                I think there may be good in this affair.
                New possibilities come into view.
                Now Romeo will get what is his due.
                Your house and his by long-held hatreds blighted
                May through your union be at last united.
                Through your alliance bloody feuds will cease
                And all will live in harmony and peace.

JULIETTE:       My heart leaps up with joy to contemplate
                The hope that Romeo may be my mate.
                But what of his tormented father's wrath,
                A fearful blockage standing in our path?
                Descending on us from the Appennines,
                With who knows what despicable designs,
                Seeking revenge on those who caused him grief,
                He may cause suffering beyond belief
                Among us. Though I know not what to fear
                His coming will be harmful, that is clear.
                However calm he seems, his rage is great.

FLAVIA:         And Madame, what would stimulate such hate?
                And even if he feels it, won't the discovery
                Of his lost son bring him a quick recovery?

JULIETTE:       If that were all, alas, but there are other
                Forces at work. My father's villainous brother
                Hated their house, and brigands in his pay
                Were those who took Montague's sons away.
                If Roger knew where Montague had fled
                He never would give up till he were dead.
                His fury might be hidden, but no doubt
                Some day its horror would have broken out.
                I do not know his plots, but I have heard

In Pisa he had but to say the word
And any sort of crime might be committed.
For him the worst excesses were permitted.
Thank Heaven he died many years ago.
But blood unites us, Flavia, and so
My life-long dread of him has not diminished.
I fear with him I never shall be finished.
When still a child, some instinct made it clear
When he approached, there was a monster near.
My heart would tremble as I fled away
And thoughts of him still trouble me today.
I hate his memory!

FLAVIA:                                    Madam I see,
But they were baseless fears that troubled me.
Of Montague's revenge we all might fear,
But that, it seems, is not what brought him here.
No troops, his only escort seems to be
A weak old man more miserable than he.
His rank he hides, and surely he'd have brought
His sons if it were conflict that he sought.
I was mistaken.

JULIETTE:                                Could I only see
My Romeo, how happy I would be.
Count Paris sought to win my hand, it's true
But I disdained his love, and he withdrew.
My father, seeking more renown to earn,
Then made my brother's wedding his concern.
If Theobald should wed as he desires,
He'd gain the rank to which he so aspires.
But, Flavia, love is my soul's desire,
My heart glows bright with its enchanting fire.
My heart and Romeo's were born to be
Bound to each other for eternity.
Could I escape the fate that holds me fast
Guilt-free, I could embrace my love at last.
How well he merits this. His noble acts
Show that my choice is based on solid facts!
He bears my image everywhere, I know
And trembling, I behold his glory grow.
His deeds make other combats petty quarrels
And I inspire his honor and his laurels.

Without my love, he never would have shown
Such greatness. Now, you must leave us alone.
He's coming.

FLAVIA *leaves*.


Scene 2

ROMEO, JULIETTE, SOLDIERS *carrying banners*.

ROMEO (*to the* SOLDIERS): Good companions, gather round.
                    Lay down your banners here upon the ground.
                    Our Prince awards me for our victories
                    The right to honor Capulet with these.
                    I'm satisfied.

*The* SOLDIERS *put down the banners and leave.*

ROMEO (*to* JULIETTE):        Madame I seek no prize
                    No joy but looking once more in your eyes.
                    What mortal, captivated by your charms,
                    Would not have carried out great feats of arms?
                    Love has sustained me; my deeds are your own,
                    And loved by you, can I remain unknown?
                    Fate seems to smile, great honors have I won,
                    But I take little pride in what I've done.
                    Over the universe I might hold sway,
                    But still the prize I seek is far away.

JULIETTE:          It's true our world small happiness affords
                    And yet our state offers us some rewards.
                    These tender conversations that we share,
                    The pleasure of your sight, however rare,
                    The concert of two hearts that must remain
                    United in woe, yet seeking to sustain
                    Their love and virtue, which provide a buffer
                    For any anguish fate may make them suffer.
                    Though I may be a Capulet by name
                    I share with Montague a common flame.
                    From earliest years my father's taken care
                    That I with pride his noble name would bear.
                    Now I abhor what he is master of

And have become a Montague through love.
This sentiment alone possesses me.

ROMEO:         But still a constant threat to us I see.
I love you Juliette, and your fair charms
Are only made more bright by these alarms.
But your attractiveness must surely be
Clear to whoever has the eyes to see.
Old Capulet (alas, I fear my fate!)
May seek to give you to some other mate
If he so barbarous a plan pursues
You still may thwart him, Juliette, if you chose.
He loves you, he's your father, he'll give way
Before your tears, which anyone would sway.
Only by this can our love be secured.
I see him.


Scene 3

CAPULET, ROMEO, JULIETTE

ROMEO:                         Lord, our triumph is assured.
To honor you these banners are on view,
The courage I have shown I owe to you,
You are my model, all to you I owe ...

CAPULET:       Your valor is exceptional, I know.
Your conquering arm has won this great effect,
Death you have spread, and earned my great respect.
Your virtuous heart has brought about all this.
Be witness now of a new source of bliss.
(to JULIETTE):
 My daughter, it delights me to relate
Count Paris has agreed to be your mate.
He's worthy of you; all will be delighted,
And by tomorrow you can be united.
I have considered everything: his birth,
How much alliances like this are worth.
You know your duty, and it's understood
You'll do my bidding, as a daughter should.

Rape and assassination in those times
Were common practice, scarcely even crimes
One party falling subsequently rose
Only to set up scaffolds for its foes.
Sons forced to watch their captured sire's demise
And infants killed before their mothers' eyes.
Some thrown to death from towers, others drowned
In the Adige, their bodies never found.
Children, their parents poisoned, orphans made,
Elderly fathers by their sons betrayed,
Ramparts demolished, sacred temples doomed,
Two thousand citizens by flames consumed,
Vengeance unleashed, the people forced to view
What barbarism uncontrolled can do.
These are the horrors that you can prevent.
Must I await for you to give consent?
The Montagues ...

ROMEO:                                    Sir, call them to assemble.
Whatever their plots, we have no need to tremble.
(*indicating the banners*)
These glorious banners, our late victory's prize
My conquering arm has placed before your eyes.
I dare do all to pacify the state,
What dangers then should we anticipate?
Before you or your daughter suffered strife
I would a hundred times lay down my life.

CAPULET:    Your noble ardor warms my heart, in truth,
I see in it the flame of my own youth.
But still, Dolvedo, age makes us more wise
I see the world now with much clearer eyes.
The state and Ferdinand owe much to you
And pour on you the glory that is due.
Now add your voice to mine, help me convince
My stubborn daughter she must wed the Prince.
I'm sure she will be swayed by your advice.
Convince her she must make this sacrifice.
Speak to her. I must go, reports are rife
Of secret dangers threatening new strife.

*He goes.*

## Scene 4

### ROMEO, JULIETTE

ROMEO:
>Losing the one I love tears at my soul,
>Must I also contribute to that goal?
>In favor of a rival must I plead,
>And so contribute to this odious deed?
>Ah! Rather let my arm express my hate
>And slay the rival who would separate
>Two happy lovers ...

JULIETTE:
>                         Do you think your wrath
>Can open to us some more hopeful path?
>What can it serve ...

ROMEO:
>                         I do not think that you
>Have any concept what great love can do.
>Your tears are few, your wishes half expressed.
>Have you a lover's heart within your breast?
>Were I in your place, Heaven!

JULIETTE:
>                         Would you dare
>Defy your father? Not his feelings spare?
>His rights ...

ROMEO:
>                         His rights, you say! What thoughtless words!
>Arc parents our defenders, or our lords?
>By what authorization can they dream
>To claim over our hearts some power supreme?
>Do we not know those hearts better than they?
>Yet they are furious when we disobey.
>These monsters ...

JULIETTE:
>                         Ah! My Lord, do not allow
>Your anger to becloud your vision now.
>I understand your sorrow; it is just.
>You feel the passion that a lover must.
>But can we at the altar stand confessing
>Our mutual love without our fathers' blessing?
>They seek our happiness; perhaps they see,
>Without our passion, more distinct than we.
>Our happiness is all they've ever sought.

Love can be feigned, paternal fondness not.
Their power is great, but it's by love restrained.
They well have earned what power they have gained.
What am I saying? Lord, your soul compares,
Though troubled now, most favorably with theirs.
Consider, though ...

ROMEO:                          Would you excuse the hand
That would make naught of everything we've planned?

JULIETTE:     Like you I tremble, but I cannot hear
You vilify the father I revere.
Do you not see the cost that he is paying
To hold fast to the firmness he's displaying?
Can we reproach him when he does not know
The tender feelings that torment us so?
He'd drag me to the altar on my knees,
But it is not the state he seeks to please.
His soul ...

ROMEO:                          Then am I wrong? Can you expect
In such a case to hold my passions checked?
Must I, born Montague, now stand aside
And see my love become my rival's bride?
Today, crowned with my enemies' defeat,
Placing my heart and glory at your feet,
Must I, oh Heaven, see before my eyes
A hated rival carry off my prize?
Acquire with ease an object of such charms,
Earned by my tears, and conquered by my arms!
True, Madame, I refuse to moderate
My passion when reduced to such a state.
Your virtue may be great, your motives pure,
But I think of the loss I must endure.
Your stoicism may enhance your fame
But you could share my sorrow all the same.

JULIETTE:     How little, dearest love, you know my heart
Think you I peacefully could see us part?
Regard ...

ROMEO:                          You weep!

JULIETTE:                        My tears so far I've kept
Within my heart, but as you spoke, I wept.
I've still preserved my honor and I feel
Outrage as well as you and equal zeal.
Have you some vision I'm unworthy of?
I have less rage perhaps, but much more love.
But let's not quarrel now, but sadly share
These last sad moments as a loving pair.
And be assured, although we now must part
No other love will ever warm my heart.

ROMEO:        My love ...

JULIETTE:                        Oh sorrow!

ROMEO:                                Strangers, can we stand it?

JULIETTE:     My father and my state alike demand it.

ROMEO:        Your charming face I never more will see!

JULIETTE:     I pray that death will shortly set me free.


Scene 5

ROMEO, JULIETTE, ALBERIC


ROMEO:        'Tis you, dear Alberic ...

ALBERIC:                        I must apprise you
Of secret happenings which will surprise you.
A wondering old man is the surprise
Who's carefully stayed hidden from our eyes.
His name is known, his mystery is clear.
'Tis Montague.

ROMEO:                        My father!

JULIETTE:                                Do I hear
Correctly?

ROMEO:                              I must run to clasp his knees.

JULIETTE:          Be calm, my love.

ALBERIC:                                    They say our enemies
Have stirred his hate and that Count Paris, fearful of their rage,
Has no desire to make a marriage vow.

ROMEO:            What joy! What unexpected news you bring
My heart leaps up! My fading hopes take wing.
Madame, can we ...

JULIETTE:                                These moments we must spend
Considering what these events portend.
Your father still does not know you are here
Let him not see you yet; don't go too near.
If you still love me, don't make any move
Til you've consulted me, and I approve.

ACT II

Scene 1

ROMEO, JULIETTE

ROMEO:     Ferdinand, Madame, answering my prayers,
           Has pledged to calmly settle our affairs.
           Our fathers reconcile, and thus maintain
           A lasting peace and concord in his reign.
           He's coming now, and Montague comes too
           And if my fondest hopes are coming true
           His gentle heart and tactful strategies
           Will reconcile these two old enemies.
           As soon as this changed situation starts
           I'll take advantage of their generous hearts,
           Their hatred fading, and their wrath abating
           I'll kneel before them, not a moment waiting.
           I will reveal my birth, and will embrace
           My father, finally in my rightful place.
           Our sacred bond, the troth that we have plighted
           Will stand as proof our houses are united.
           And still amid my joy I must confess
           I feel a touch of fear, some slight distress.
           I leave you knowing not what to expect
           To meet a father whom I much respect
           But do not know. The wrongs he has endured
           May have left wounds that won't be quickly cured.
           Many a tear I've shed, to contemplate
           His isolated and abandoned state.
           For he has had to bear his grief alone;
           The fate of my two brothers is unknown.
           But our reunion will bring some redress;
           And my own happiness he'll surely bless.
           Heaven at last has given us our due.

JULIETTE:  But one request, my love, I make of you.

ROMEO:     Request! Oh Heaven! Know that I would take
           For law any request that you might make.

JULIETTE:  When you meet Montague, doubtless your blood
           Will feel attraction to him, as it should.

And in that instant, when has been revealed
Your kinship with him, now so long concealed,
If he should still maintain his hate, denying
The peaceful efforts Ferdinand is trying,
You as his son will have no other path
Than to unite with him and share his wrath.
If he concedes, then all our woes are passed.
If he does not, then hold our secret fast.
Will you do this?

ROMEO:                              I will.

JULIETTE:                                   This moment, now
You'll take my hands and solemnize this vow?

ROMEO:          I swear by all the love I bear for you,
That to your law I'll be forever true.
If Heaven strikes me, to my rival bear
The tenderness that we this moment share.

JULIETTE:       I am content. But see! My father's here.

FERDINAND (*to* CAPULET): Montague's suffering is all too clear.
                 I urge you Capulet, to show some pity
                 For this unhappy pilgrim to our city.
                 See in what piteous state he has arrived.

CAPULET:        I pity him the ills he has survived,
But I have rights as well, and far from ceding ...

FERDINAND:      We don't yet know for what he may be pleading.
Compare your fates; you have a daughter fair
A happy family, a son and heir,
Prepared to wed, your needs to gratify
And raise the glory of your family high.
Let Montague's unhappy state remind you
Whate'er your height, misfortune still can find you.
He comes.

## Scene 2

FERDINAND, MONTAGUE, CAPULET, ROMEO, JULIETTE, SOLDIERS of FERDINAND, COURTESANS, OFFICERS, *leading* MONTAGUE.

MONTAGUE (*to the* OFFICERS *conducting him*): Cruel ones! Where are you
                    taking me? What is this place. What's your authority?
                    (*to* FERDINAND): Who's this?
FERDINAND:      Your Duke! There is no reason for alarm.
                    I've never sought to do you any harm.
                    I've brought you here in hopes I may undo
                    The feud between the Capulets and you.

MONTAGUE:      The Capulets! Oh God!

FERDINAND:                           Why such concern?
                    In members of my suite do you discern
                    Some enemy who bears you some ill will?

MONTAGUE (*pointing to* CAPULET):
                    He's there! Who hates me and my family
                    still.

CAPULET:             You recognize me through your hate and I
                    Feel my own hatred rising in reply.

FERDINAND (*to* CAPULET):
                    Wait, Capulet, be not so unforgiving.
                    (*to* MONTAGUE):
                    Montague, answer. How have you been living?
                    Hidden in savage woods, in abject state,
                    Is that the proper lot of one so great?
                    Have you renounced my realm and all its goods?

MONTAGUE:      Think you that life's so hard within those woods?

FERDINAND:      But you, brought up in ease and luxury,
                    What charm is there?

MONTAGUE:                        Mankind no more to see.

FERDINAND:      Mankind is so offensive to your eyes?

MONTAGUE:    Who sees them clearly cannot but despise.

FERDINAND:    Those woods have hardened you and fed your wrath.

MONTAGUE:    Not so, your court confirmed me on this path.

FERDINAND:    Your children ...

MONTAGUE:                        Stop. Of them I will not speak.

FERDINAND:    Then are they safe?

MONTAGUE:                            For them in vain you'll seek.

FERDINAND:    Their fate ...

MONTAGUE:                        I've spoken. Leave this mystery.

FERDINAND:    I will respect your secret, as you'll see.
But can I without sorrow contemplate
So great a soul languish in such a state?
Take back your former glory and your rank.

MONTAGUE:    I do not need them.

FERDINAND:                            What have we to thank
For this despair which rules your troubled mind?

MONTAGUE:    Unhappiness.

FERDINAND:                        Some treatment will we find.
(*louder*) Within my court we will forget the past
And lift the shadows suffering has cast.
The Capulets hold no more hate for you.

CAPULET:    Can I refuse the pity that is due?

MONTAGUE:    Pity? Great God! Fom you? Is that my lot
Give me your hate ten-fold! Pity me not!

CAPULET:    He must be humored.

MONTAGUE:                                        That's what I desire.
                        Your peaceful words will not put out my fire.
                        Between our houses war eternal reigns.

CAPULET:          The gods will choose who loses and who gains.

MONTAGUE:        It is not victory that will complete
                        My happiness, but rather your defeat.

CAPULET:          Go then, cruel man ...

MONTAGUE:                                        No more than you.

CAPULET:          My party reigns.

MONTAGUE:                              That can change too.

CAPULET:          Enough.

MONTAGUE:                            Your choice.

FERDINAND:                                    What! Now, before my eyes
                        You'll let such odious excesses arise?
                        Before me here, you'd both let loose such hate
                        As to create a menace to our state?
                        Who is the enemy that would attack?
                        What forts must I equip to hold him back?
                        It's you who menace fair Verona's peace
                        Your lust for vengeance, which you cannot cease.
                        Your pride, your disobedience are the core
                        Of conflicts that could lead to civil war!
                        What progress did our recent triumphs gain
                        If your disputes bring suffering again?
                        Your hearts are noble, can you think it good
                        To ope again our tombs and shed our blood?
                        Montague, Capulet, both men of worth
                        Have pity on the land that gave you birth.
                        I speak as citizen and not as lord.
                        My people are my all, spare them the sword.

ROMEO (*to* MONTAGUE): My Lord, be calm, and master your offenses.
                        Your great misfortune everyone here senses.
                        But your high spirit can subdue its hate,

|              | And bring to all a peaceful, happy fate.<br>Capulet honors you, and I would show<br>Toward you the love I to a father owe. |
|--------------|---|
| JULIETTE:    | And on my knees I swear to you, my Lord.<br>Between us there shall be no more discord.<br>And if my father's actions caused you pain<br>We will all strive to make it right again. |
| FERDINAND:   | Despite yourself your tears flow, Montague. |
| MONTAGUE:    | I weep with pain and anger, that is true.<br>That is his daughter. |
| FERDINAND:   | Come, deign to forgive. |
| ROMEO:       | Forget your wrongs. |
| JULIETTE:    | Allow yourself to live. |
| MONTAGUE:    | I'll live! |
| FERDINAND:   | What hidden motive can impede you? |
| ROMEO:       | Why keep your silence? |
| JULIETTE:    | Speak. We all will heed you. |
| FERDINAND:   | Inform me ... |

MONTAGUE (*placing his hand on his breast*): I will not. My grief's my own.
　　　　　　　To no one else it ever will be known.

| FERDINAND:   | Madman! |
|--------------|---|
| MONTAGUE:    | Perhaps, but seek not to appease me.<br>I'll hate whoever sets about to please me.<br>I spurn your court, your Caputlets, and all<br>That would ignore my anger and my fall.<br>(*pointing to* CAPULET) Yes, since my heart resolves to hate you still<br>I'll make my heart's desire my firmest will.<br>(*to the* DUKE): Go, take elsewhere your favor and your pleas, |

But your high rank may have its own disease.
You think yourself against all crime a buffer.
You could be wrong, and innocents will suffer.
I'll say no more, but here I will remain,
And gladly bear the horror and the pain
My hatred and my rage, my anguish too,
Knowing that they will also burden you.
As for the Capulets, may Heaven devise
Torments for them that will delight my eyes.
Let loose your fury on them, let my plight
Spur you to chastise them with all your might!

FERDINAND:    Guards, come to me!

ROMEO:    Lord, what do you propose?

JULIETTE:    Consider his white hairs, respect his woes.

FERDINAND:    Enough. I've spoken.

MONTAGUE:    Villains! Now hold back
Or let me die under your cruel attack.

FERDINAND (*to the* GUARDS): Guard the old man with care.
    (*to* CAPULET *and* MONTAGUE): Perhaps you planned
That I would cede to you the upper hand.
I have the power, and will not tolerate
Your plots that might destabilize the state.
Guards, keep him here a moment, I may still
Relent if he but softens his iron will.
If not, whoever so defies our power
Whate'er his party, take him to the Tower.

MONTAGUE:    The Tower! 'Neath my feet is an abyss!
But tremble, Prince, I'll be avenged for this.

CAPULET *leaves*.

FERDINAND:    Guards, render him the honor and respect
One of his age and sorrow can expect.

ROMEO:    Grant me, my Lord, permission to remain
With this old man to try to ease his pain.

FERDINAND:     You have my leave.


## Scene 3

### MONTAGUE, ROMEO


ROMEO:                                  Allow me on my knees
To some degree your sufferings appease.
I share your sorrow and will do my best
To ease their violence and bring you rest.
Did I not see you on a sudden cower
At Ferdinand's mere mention of the Tower?

MONTAGUE:     Leave me, young man.

ROMEO:                                  Your fate is grim, I know
But he is not inflexible and so
A word from you ...

MONTAGUE (*pointing at the flags*):     Whose flags are these I see?

ROMEO:     They are the fruits of my late victory.
In that last battle ...

MONTAGUE:                                  Courage I revere.
Who are you then?

ROMEO:                                  Only what I appear—
A simple soldier risen from the ranks,
An outcast, home and family both blanks,
Now brought to tears in hearing of your harms.

MONTAGUE:     His features and his discourse have their charms.
You pity my distress?

ROMEO:                                  How could I not,
Since you and I share an unhappy lot.
MONTAGUE:     I'm moved by him.

ROMEO:                                  Aye, Sir, my heart is trembling,
My tender heart which won't abide dissembling.

All human suffering strikes me to the core.
Pity ...

MONTAGUE:          Your suffering I can't ignore.

ROMEO:          Still do I dream of an existence fairer.

MONTAGUE:          Long may you flourish in that soothing error.
These happy days will soon be in the past.

ROMEO:          But I have other comforts that will last.

MONTAGUE:          Young man, you will forgive my skepticism
Imprudently you look through hope's bright prism
Before you paths of happy promise beckon
But on the human heart you do not reckon.
You have not looked into its dark abyss
Its crime, its falseness, you know naught of this.
How pride and passions can possession take
And leave ferocious ruin in their wake.

ROMEO:          No, Sir, yet kindly Nature I am sure
Bids us to love, with ardor sweet and pure.
Above all, I am certain that affection
Has guided me just now in your direction.
I've fought for you, rushing to undertake
Whatever I am able for your sake.
Accept then my embraces as revealing
A simple heart giv'n over to natural feeling.
To you I swear devotion and respect
As coming from your son you would expect.
I will respect your sorrows as my own
Mingle my tears with yours, and with you groan.
But why abandon hope, you surely see,
Better than I, how fickle fate can be.
Perhaps great happiness will be your fate
Bear your indignities and calmly wait.
Believe that ... but I see the ducal power
Come to conduct you to the fearful Tower ...

MONTAGUE (*to the* GUARDS, *joining them*):I'm ready.

ROMEO:          Wait ...

MONTAGUE:                    Friend, to yourself attend.
                    Find happiness, for mine is at an end.

*The* SOLDIERS *lead out* MONTAGUE.


## Scene 4

### ROMEO, JULIETTE

ROMEO (*to the* GUARDS *who are leading away* MONTAGUE):
                    To what a cruel constraint this poor man bows!

JULIETTE:        But has your heart been faithful to your vows?
                    Did you remember ...

ROMEO:                                      Ah, my oath unwise
                    And barbarous! He is ta'en before my eyes.

JULIETTE:        All would be lost had you not silent kept.

ROMEO:           And now my father in chains I must accept.


## Scene 5

### ROMEO, JULIETTE, FLAVIA

FLAVIA:          Madam, old Montague still has supporters
                    Who will release him from his prison quarters.
                    And we all fear that once he is set free
                    Sooner or later Capulet and he
                    Will meet and deadly battle will ensue
                    Killing the one, the other, or the two.
                    We fear for you and yours, for Capulet.

JULIETTE:        Must my love against my father set!
                    I fear for such a combat. Can you not,
                    My Lord, cut through this net in which we're caught.
                    My Capulet, Thebaldo ...

## Scene 6

### ROMEO, JULIETTE, ALBERIC, FLAVIA

ALBERIC:                                   Madam, know
Your father, filled with rage against his foe,
Aroused by tauntings he could not abide
Claiming he dares not show his face outside
Has left his palace, giving them the lie
And with your brother, he is now close by.

JULIETTE:        I run to stop them.

*She leaves with* FLAVIA.

## Scene 7

### ROMEO, ALBERIC

ROMEO:        Follow me, my friend. I'll fight with you,
and your just cause defend.

## ACT III

### Scene 1

### ROMEO, ALBERIC

ALBERIC:     Where are you going? Danger thither lies.

ROMEO:     To Juliette, to die before her eyes.

ALBERIC:     Have you forgotten 'twas your hand, no other
That even now deprived her of a brother?
That with that very blood your sword is rank?

ROMEO:     Have pity, friend. Plunge it in my own flank!

ALBERIC:     Come, leave! The untoward actions of your hand
In time perhaps your love will understand.
For now spare her the knowledge that her lover
Has killed her brother. First let her recover.
Thank heaven I alone was there to see
The fearful progress of this tragedy.
Do not give way before these frightful blows!

ROMEO:     And will his sister perish when she knows?

ALBERIC:     Now you must flee, from their revenge to hide.

ROMEO:     Without his death my father would have died.
But what a price, what sacrifice I gave.
Alas!

ALBERIC:                    He's dead. Now strive yourself to save.
Your love and Capulet will soon be here.
Master your feelings, let no stress appear.

ROMEO:     'Tis she. Be gone.

ALBERIC *leaves.*

## Scene 2

### ROMEO, JULIETTE

JULIETTE:                                Romeo, it is I.
With fiercely burning heart to you I fly.
Your heart, I know, weeps for your father's ill
And that great anger that consumes him still!
But though our land with bitterness is rife
So far our love has kept above this strife.
Yet of your suffering I am aware
And of this burden I would take my share.
Think of my love and let me beg you whether
It were not better we should grieve together.
For lovers united in a love they treasure
Weeping together can give gentle pleasure.
Let Juliette sooth you to sweet repose.

ROMEO:       Alas, how Heaven multiplies our woes!

JULIETTE:    Are there new threats? What dangers do you see?

ROMEO:       I fear a storm. Dark is our destiny.

JULIETTE:    We shall prevail.

ROMEO:                    Perhaps.

JULIETTE:                            What should we fear?
Your virtues, your accomplishments are clear.
The Duke admires you, and my father ranks
You with my brother in his praise and thanks.
My brother loves you too, you are aware
He would with pleasure all your burdens share.
He'd die for you and never count the cost.

ROMEO:       On those same terms would that my life were lost!

JULIETTE:    When one heart thus seeks out another heart
What cruel fate would keep them thus apart?

ROMEO:       Perhaps our warring fathers, catching sight
Of our distress, will hold in check their fight.

JULIETTE:    This happy outcome seems far distant still
But nature and our tears may bend their will.
Their crimes have not yet touched us, we remain
Free of their wrath, and of their hatred's stain.
Rightly or wrongly, we our love have plighted
My heart dreams of the day we are united.
You know that I adore you, my proud sire,
Bouyed by his offspring's joy, will cool his ire.
His son especially, in wedded bliss,
Will do a great deal to accomplish this.
What happiness for all of those I love!


## Scene 3

### ROMEO, JULIETTE, FLAVIA

FLAVIA:    Madame, ill news ...

JULIETTE:                                                        What's this? Oh, heavens above!
My spirit fails. Be quick, tell me the worst.

FLAVIA:    Cruel Montague has from his prison burst,
His friends broke down the gates, and scarcely free
He took advantage of his liberty
To track down Capulet, and in a breath
Engaged him in a battle to the death.
Your father clearly saw his end in sight
When suddenly your brother joined the fight.
Then a new figure lept into the fray.
He killed your brother and then fled away.

JULIETTE:    Who's this assassin?

FLAVIA:                                                Madame, no one knows.

JULIETTE:    My father ...

FLAVIA:                                    Now is added to his woes
The loss of his dear son. His groans resound.
He swears revenge when the assassin's found.

JULIETTE:     My dear Thebaldo. Flavia, please go.

FLAVIA *goes.*

## Scene 4

### ROMEO, JULIETTE

JULIETTE:     I am consumed with grief, my Romeo!
              Heavens! My brother dead! Me broken-hearted!
              Weep with me for your friend so soon departed.
              My dreamed-of happiness is flown away.
              What monster could so good a person slay?
              Dear brother, when we bid our last goodbye,
              How could I dream you were about to die?
              I see, dear Romeo, your looks reveal
              That you are sharing in the grief I feel.
              Who else but you, companion of this grief,
              Could share my tears and bring me some relief?
              This blow, though fearful, devastates me less,
              Since I have your support in my distress.
              Heavens! You tremble and seem loathe to face me.

ROMEO:        For pity, let me go. Do not embrace me.

JULIETTE:     Why this withdrawal? Why this silence?  Let
              Me learn ...

ROMEO:                          Ye gods!

JULIETTE:                             Romeo!

ROMEO:                                      Juliette!

JULIETTE:     Barbarian! You have my brother killed!

ROMEO:        Tear out my heart and let your wrath be stilled.

JULIETTE:     Heavens!

ROMEO:                          You wish my death?

JULIETTE:                                    Oh cruel one ... I ...

ROMEO (*laying his hand on his sword*): Say but the word and on that word I die.

JULIETTE:        What have you done?

ROMEO:                                    What other could I do?
                My father was expiring in my view.
                Duty demanded I do as I ought
                And pushed all other matters from my thought.
                I ran, I thrust. My own love I let go
                To save his life to whom my life I owe.
                Your love I have betrayed, your hopes denied
                But with all this, I'm not a parricide.
                I hold myself in scorn and realize
                That I am now offensive to your eyes.
                The courage of the Montagues I've shown
                The Capulets must now present their own.
                Your father's wrath must now on me descend
                Unarmed I'll meet him, and accept my end.
                Defenseless I'll surrender unto him
                This bloody sword as a reminder grim,
                And I will die content, if by this deed
                I offer you the justice that you need.

JULIETTE:        Do not add your own death to all this strife!
                Barbarous one, I tremble for your life!
                What powerful attraction through my grief
                Drives me to seek in you alone relief?
                Pardon me my dear brother, but you knew
                About our love. It was approved by you.
                Perhaps you tremble at the thought that I'd
                Forgive the person at whose hand you died.
                Ah, Romeo, if it be Heaven's will
                I too shall die, because I love you still.
                Take my life too, or somehow help me fight
                The guilty joy I feel within your sight.
                We now must part. We have but little time
                Before my father finds who did this crime.
                You still have time his awful wrath to flee;
                And put between us rivers, mountains, sea.
                Be sure although we must forever part
                You always will remain in Juliette's heart.

My love will follow you, wherever you stray,
Wherever you behold the light of day.
Do not wait here where I will see you taken.
Give me your life, although I am forsaken.
I am resolved in this, whatever the cost,
Though both a love and brother I have lost.


## Scene 5

### CAPULET, ROMEO, JULIETTE

CAPULET:        Dolvedo, follow me. My son is dead.
                Revenge must fall on the assassin's head.

ROMEO (*aside*): Who's that? Ye gods!

CAPULET:                                I did not see his face.
                But Montague ...

ROMEO:                  What? He?

CAPULET:                                Planned this disgrace.
                Friend and avenger, my hopes lie in you.
                My tears you see, my blanched locks you view.
                Your courage you have proven by your deeds,
                You are the champion my family needs.
                These arms, now trembling with rage and grief
                Lack still the victim who would bring relief.
                Find Montague, kill him, and bring the prize
                Of his still beating heart before my eyes.
                My gratitude to you will know no end,
                You will become my son, my bosom friend.
                Go, and gain victory at any cost
                And you'll replace the son that I have lost.

ROMEO:          What are you asking?

CAPULET:                                Why this hesitation?
                You clearly view my plea with reservation.

ROMEO:          Ah, Heaven!

CAPULET:                            Enough. My daughter, come with me.
                 Vainly I put my trust in him, I see.
                 I am ashamed for both of us that I
                 Thought on your coward's heart I could rely.
                 Go to Count Paris, who is known
                 To favor strong ambition like your own.
                 Risk death for him, if that is your desire.
                 (*to* JULIETTE):
                 Come, follow.

JULIETTE:                          Lord ...

CAPULET:                             You tremble!

JULIETTE:                                        Oh, my Sire!

CAPULET:         A strong suspicion bursts upon my sight!
                 Why this confused embarrassment, this fright?

JULIETTE:        Ah, Heaven!

CAPULET:                          In my family's bosom may
                 A foul seducer ta'en my jewel as prey?
                 Has this unworthy love made you oppose
                 The mate for you that your own father chose ...

JULIETTE:        I'm lost!

CAPULET:                 You blush? Can you so guilty be?

JULIETTE:        Lord ...

CAPULET:                 If I thought ...

JULIETTE:                             I pray ...

CAPULET (*laying his hand on his sword*):           A traitor, she!

ROMEO:           Stay, Capulet, hear me. Let me reveal
                 The rightful object of the rage you feel.
                 'Twas you who in this fearful monster trusted,
                 This ingrate who after your daughter lusted,

The son of your worst foe, old Montague.
Romeo.

JULIETTE: All is lost!

CAPULET: Can this be true?

ROMEO: Hear all my faults. This crimson hand you see,
Drips with her brother's blood, blood shed by me.

CAPULET: My son!

JULIETTE: Alas!

CAPULET: Fiend! No more can I bear!
Defend yourself.

ROMEO: My heart is yours. Strike there.

JULIETTE: Stop this.

CAPULET: Defend yourself.

ROMEO: Set free your ire.
I had to kill your son to save my sire.

JULIETTE: Stop.

CAPULET: Wretched daughter, do not seek to stay
My arm, my just revenge must have its way.
Coward, you know full well what an offense
It is to strike a man without defense.
Go then, and save yourself in shameful flight
Remove your odious presence from my sight.


## Scene 6

### CAPULET, ROMEO, JULIETTE, an OFFICER OF THE DUKE

OFFICER: The Duke of your new loss and suffering knows
And will do what he can to ease your woes.
He's coming to console you in this hour.

CAPULET:        I do not want his pity but his power.
                (*to* ROMEO) You'll not escape me, henceforth every breath
                I take, I will by all means seek your death.
                (*to his daughter*):
                Follow me.

*He leaves.*

ROMEO:                          Speak, my love! What can we do?

JULIETTE:       We'll die together or I'll live for you.

ACT IV

Scene 1

FERDINAND, CAPULET

FERDINAND:     Capulet, with your woes I sympathize
Whatever reason says, tears must arise.
We're suffering humans but our woes are not
Relieved when to them new woes we have brought.
If your rebellious child should not survive,
Your house is lost which she might yet revive.
Pardon her.

CAPULET:                              Prince, I pray, entreat me not
My son ...

FERDINAND:                      Can our regret for him do aught?
You have loved Romeo, your better sense
I trust to speak in you in his defense.
I honor these paternal tears you've shed
And will in tribute to the son who's dead
Bestow on you all honors that the city
Gives to its greatest ...

CAPULET:                              Stop, my Lord, for pity.

FERDINAND:     Let me in any case your sorrows share
This is the burden that all men must bear.
Do not think you are singled out for woe,
It is the common lot, as well you know.
How often have my own eyes flowed with tears!
And everywhere I see good cause for fears.
The Duke of Mantua I know full well
Strives to incite my subjects to rebel.
He seeks my downfall and it would delight
Him if your houses' feud would reignite.
If Montagues and Capulets should strive
To slay each other, Mantua would thrive.
His conquering armies soon would be employed
To seize our sundered nation, self-destroyed.
Extinguish then these flames of rage and hate
That have brought ceaseless discord to our state.

You have one daughter, Montague a son
Allow their marriage; make your houses one.
Your weeping country, speaking with my voice
Implores you on its knees to make this choice.
This act will place no blot upon your name
But by its virtue will increase your fame.
One day they'll say: "Though wronged, Capulet laid
Aside revenge, his nobler side displayed,
Subdued his righteous rage and stayed his hand,
Obeyed his Prince, and saved our fatherland.
The interest of the state ruled over all."

CAPULET:       Thus Montague will triumph and I fall.

FERDINAND:     The triumph will be yours. Old Montague
Has shown he feels some sympathy for you.
The restoration of his son has brought
A moderation to his deeds and thought.
When I discovered Romeo's true name,
At once I called his father, and he came.
Brought face to face the father and his child
Shared their past stories and were reconciled.
Nature has spoken, blood has made its claim
Tenderly crying these two are the same.
My tears o'erflowed, and they importuned me
To beg you to extend them clemency;
Extend to them forgiveness, they implore you.
I told them that they must appear before you.
They're here.

CAPULET:                    Good Lord!

FERDINAND:                              As citizen be true!


Scene 2

FERDINAND, MONTAGUE, CAPULET, ROMEO

FERDINAND:     Come forward then, fear nothing, Montague.
Capulet pardons you.

MONTAGUE:                                    Gods, can it be?
              Over yourself have you won victory?
              Your heart has softened?

CAPULET:                                  Yes, it has. That's true.
              But still my pardon little does for you.

FERDINAND:    Think rather your forgiveness is a call
              To stir the clemency that lies in all.

ROMEO (*to the* DUKE): My Prince!
              (*to* MONTAGUE): My father!
              (*falling at* CAPULET's *feet*): For what you have done,
              Allow me to embrace you as a son.

CAPULET:      What, Romeo?

MONTAGUE:                         Accept his flowing tears.

CAPULET:      Delight can spring from hatred, it appears.

MONTAGUE:     Vengeance I see you truly have forsaken.
              Hatred has melted.

CAPULET:                               You are not mistaken.
              Pity will rule my heart instead of hate,
              And both of us will live now for the state.

MONTAGUE:     I join my vows to yours.

FERDINAND:                            Friends, let us go.
              And this new concord to the people show.
              Among these tombs, among these oaks and ferns.
              Where sleep our ancestors in marble urns,
              Before the people and myself renew
              The vow of people just taken here by you.
              Swear on these sepulchers, these vaults so dark
              The names and ashes gathered in this park
              To turn against our enemies the wrath
              That once led us on a divisive path.
              To forge between us an august alliance
              Friendship at home and to our foes, defiance!
              And warriors once involved in civil strife

Will now unite to give our state new life.
Thus women, children, all our grateful nation
Will celebrate your reconciliation.
My subjects, teardrops flowing from their eyes,
Will praise your houses' virtues to the skies.
Murder and plots are past. It is to you
The credit for our future fame is due.
It shall be my concern while I still reign,
From citizens like you respect to gain.
You're moved, I see. You sigh, your eyes are wet.

MONTAGUE:    Shall we unite our houses, Capulet?

FERDINAND:    I'll answer for his heart. 'Tis one with you.

CAPULET:    See what you have accomplished, Montague.
The state, my sovereign, have achieved this peace.
The cry of blood may now its clamor cease.
But since that cry is still not fully stilled
Yet one more pardon still must be fulfilled.
You have a son, while my son breathes no more,
His cries for vengeance now I must ignore.
In this day, in this place, let bloodshed cease
His murderers and I embrace in peace.
My hatred, Montague, like yours is done,
I dare to clasp the hand of this, your son.
Is this enough to prove to you that I
Am now a friend on whom you can rely?
As enemy I swore your days to end
But now I will protect them, as a friend.
You have obtained my friendship at small cost;
I weep when I remember all I've lost.
But I will pledge I'll make your son my own
Though by his hand my son was overthrown.

ROMEO:    My Lord! My father! How can I repay
The blessings you have heaped on me today?

## Scene 3

### FERDINAND, MONTAGUE, CAPULET, ROMEO, AN OFFICER

OFFICER:        My Lord, those villains whom your state abuse
                Seeking for some occasion they can use
                Are growing stronger, and they may soon move,
                To challenge you and your regime remove.
                I fear ...

FERDINAND:              It is enough. My diligence
                Forsaw this. All is ready for defense.
                I go. You, Capulet, my soldiers lead.

*He goes out with the* OFFICER.


## Scene 4

### MONTAGUE, CAPULET, ROMEO

CAPULET:        Someone to guard my house and home I need.
                (*to* MONTAGUE):  As ruler of my house, I pray, stay here,
                I leave my daughter with you without fear.
                In love and hate I take no half-way stands,
                All that I have I leave here in your hands.
                And if (a possibility my heart denies)
                The slightest anger still in your heart lies,
                My trust in you I surely have made clear
                By placing in your hands all I hold dear.

*He goes.*


## Scene 5

### MONTAGUE, ROMEO

ROMEO:          May lightning strike us should we e'er betray
                The harmony that we have sealed this day!

MONTAGUE:       As you my son?

ROMEO:                     My Lord, some fear I feel.

MONTAGUE:     Do you foresee the secrets I'll reveal?

ROMEO:     What secrets?

MONTAGUE:                         Listen. As you are a man
Rally whatever fortitude you can.
You'll tremble at the news I must reveal.

ROMEO:     Speak.

MONTAGUE:          Do not move. Be firm and fast as steel.
Without suspecting fearful mystery what you sought of late
You asked me to reveal your brothers' fate.
They are no more.

ROMEO:                              Ye gods!

MONTAGUE:                                  Far from this place,
I sought with them a refuge by the grace
Of Pisa. There I thought would be no strife
My sons and I could lead a tranquil life.
No enemies were there, no traps awaited,
But vengeance followed, unanticipated.
A foe implacable had me accused
Of some false plot, and unaware, abused,
And with no chance to answer to his lie
I was shut in a tower, there to die.

ROMEO:     And your sons too?

MONTAGUE:                          Them too. Now hear the rest.
For three days I remained that dark cell's guest.
Then a fresh terror came to trouble me.
I dreamed what seemed a fearful prophecy
Of horrible destruction and disaster.
I sprang awake, my poor heart beating faster,
And tried to think, my body tense and cold,
What awful fate this fearful dream foretold.
My children slept, I ran to them. Their sight
Did not becalm, but added to my fright.
In hunger they lay gasping on their bed
And "father" through their tears they weakly said.
Surely, we thought, someone would soon arrive,

And give us crumbs at least to stay alive.
We silent were. I listened, but I heard
Within that tower nothing, not a word.
My children I laid out, held back my tears,
They wept, I agonized, but hid my fears.
And when at last (oh gods, could you stand by?)
I saw them one by one weaken and die,
I gnawed my hands. Renaud, with dying breath,
Said "Father, swear you will avenge my death."
The others offered blood to nourish me
And each one breathed his last, each ceased to be.

ROMEO:          What have I heard! Great God!

MONTAGUE:                              The end is near.
I lived, but robbed of all that makes life dear.
I blindly rushed about my cell at first
Wanting to die of hunger and of thirst.
With funeral cries my lifeless sons I clasped
Wrestled with shadows, weeped and raged and gasped.
Always returning to stretch out beside
My sons unmoving, lying where they died.
Then suddenly, my door flew open, friends
Had come to save me  ...

ROMEO:                              But that monster's ends
Were won. He must be paid for his foul crime.

MONTAGUE:          He had not children, and I had no time.
Though weak with hunger, pausing not to rest
I ran to tear his heart out from his breast.
But came too late. The monster had just died
Happy and tranquil, stuffed with goods and pride.

ROMEO:          Are you then blocked from vengeance on your foes?

MONTAGUE:          Redress lies closer than you may suppose.

ROMEO:          Your cause is mine. You've but to point the way.

MONTAGUE:          Perhaps to strike the blow you may delay.

ROMEO:          Who must I strike?

MONTAGUE:                               The villain is no other
Than my oppressor's equally dark brother,
Capulet.

ROMEO:                     He!

MONTAGUE:                        Indeed.

ROMEO:                                Cruel fate, I pray,
Change either this assassin or this prey.

MONTAGUE:     No, it is not his blood that I want shed
But blood from one he cherishes instead.
One whom he loves to such a great extent
That if her heart is pierced, his own is rent.
In her alone his family survives,
In killing her, you terminate both lives.
'Tis Juliette.

ROMEO:                          Sir, I'm profoundly torn.
For Juliette and I are lovers sworn.

MONTAGUE:     Do you not fear the wrath that you inspire
In me by your unspeakable desire?

ROMEO:     Consider whom you're asking me to kill—
My love ... Her father ...

MONTAGUE:                      I will have my will!

ROMEO:     What have they done?

MONTAGUE:                   Great God! What have they done?
Can you ask this and still remain my son?
The blood that killed my sons flows in their veins
What childish sentiment your arm restrains?
What have they done? Do tigers so inquire
When savage darts have brought about their ire?
This family such tortures did devise
As letting my sons die before my eyes.
What have they done? Go ask your brothers that
As hunger on their dying bodies sat.
Sealed in that fatal cell, could they suppose

That their own father would forgive their foes?
What have they done? Traitor, can you deny
At my own feet I saw your brothers die.
I alone heard them, gasping, seek to give
Their blood to me, allowing me to live.
What have they done? Barbarian, I see
Heaven has taken my last hope from me.
To find that monster was my soul desire,
To see him suffer and at last expire,
To see the torture of my sons repeated
In his own pain, 'til justice was completed.
But he escaped me and now rests in peace
Within his tomb, denying my release.
Now when I find a son famed for his deeds
Seeming the perfect hero for my needs,
Who could the Capulets exterminate
With but one blow, how can he hesitate?
Unworthy sympathies hold him in thrall.
Like weighty chains. He cannot move at all.
And rather than rushing to unite our fates,
And serve his father, he deliberates!

ROMEO:      These are most cruel reproaches that you give.
I'd die a thousand times to let you live.
Unhappy man! Have you not thought about
The crimes that you would have me carry out?
My dear friend, killed by me, scarcely at rest
A peace just now achieved, thanks to the blest
Actions of an old enemy, whose trust is clear
By pledging to you all that he holds dear.
His only daughter in your trust he left,
Could you then kill her, leaving him bereft?
I just embraced him and my love expressed;
Should my sword now ravage his daughter's breast?
I am a soldier, sir. Your wrongs to right,
I pledge to you my courage and my might.
This hand from evil always has refrained
Though with the blood of enemies 'tis stained.
If honorable vengeance is the goal
There Romeo is with you, heart and soul.
To serve one's father's cause is right and fit
But not in crime, this I cannot commit.

MONTAGUE:    What do I hear? My miseries increase!
Can your poor brothers never rest in peace?
Will all betray their cause and their demand
For vengeance be betrayed on every hand?
How shall I bear the life that I have left?
Have I borne you but to be thus bereft?
When from that fatal tower at last I fled
Can you imagine what a life I led?
Full twenty years I wandered without pause
In savage, far-off lands, knowing no laws.
Deep in the mountains, haunted by nameless fears
A fugitive, I hid for many years.
Shunned even by nature, with no inclination
To ever set my feet back toward my nation.
My grief-bestricken mind retained no trace
Of home or homeland, family or race.
Sheltered by some poor soul who saw in me
A brother in his own dark misery.
Nourished by him, with every faltering breath
Making but half-formed words invoking death,
Crushed down by my vile fortune, I would lie
'Neath a malevolent, uncaring sky.
In frightful wastelands, which all mankind shuns
I'd shriek the names of my unhappy sons.
Unfeeling nature left me in my grief
No peaceful slumber ever gave relief.
Then suddenly, to my enormous fright.
My four dead sons appeared to me one night ...
I thought them there ... with healthy life aglow ...
Their faces ...

ROMEO:                          Father, let these spectres go!

MONTAGUE:    You gods! I've suffered these torments for years;
Take heed of my white locks, dry up my tears.

ROMEO:    Oh Heaven!

MONTAGUE:                          It is time. Give me my peace.
In death I'll see my sons. Grant me release.
My strength is fading ...

ROMEO:                               Take my arm, I pray ...

MONTAGUE:    Keep far from me, or else do what I say!

ROMEO:    My Lord!

MONTAGUE:    My children!

ROMEO:    In your profound pain
Think that ...

MONTAGUE:    My children!

ROMEO:    Think that I remain.

MONTAGUE:    My children! ... Where are they?

ROMEO:    Lord, I implore you,
Recall one living son still stands before you.

MONTAGUE:    What! You?

ROMEO:    Live still. Let me your hopes restore.

MONTAGUE:    I am a wretch. Existence I abhor.
There is no place for me upon this earth.

ROMEO:    What is your sin?

MONTAGUE:    To not have died at birth.

ROMEO:    Sir, you have wept enough, let dry your tears.
My brothers have been lost for many years.

MONTAGUE:    Calm reason, Romeo, comes to your aid
It is not in your blood that they have stayed;
Your heart can bear those fearful losses lightly,
A father groans from such distresses nightly.
Your brothers' trembling hands clutch not your heart
From vengeance you can hold yourself apart.
You wretched Capulets can live in peace,
But your dead victims haunt me without cease.
In their torn flesh my own existence dies.
I see tears flowing from their shuttered eyes.
When will I soften, when my curse recall?

When justice has been done unto them all.
I swear, oh Heaven, bloody deeds you'll see
In payment for the evils done to me.

ROMEO :      Think not of murder or of parricide!

MONTAGUE:    Words such as these I scorn, and push aside.
My faith has long since sunk into despair;
These words, once feared, are now but empty air.
The passion that I feel does not engage you?
Seeing a Capulet does not enrage you?
You see him as a man, and not a danger?

ROMEO:       If he's a man, he cannot be a stranger!
At last I see I must reveal the truth,
Confessing who protected me in youth.
Would you demand, your ingrate son to harm
The man who gave him his supporting arm?
Should I my childhood benefactor slay
While you discreetly turned your eyes away?
Could you betray justice, humanity,
Heaven, your faith ...

MONTAGUE:                         They were betrayed for me.

ROMEO:       Change matters then, turn evil into good.
Honor demands ...

MONTAGUE:               Revenge.

ROMEO:                                  Charity.

MONTAGUE:                                        Blood.

ROMEO:       What would you do?

MONTAGUE:                  I will this moment seize ...

ROMEO:       For the last time I beg you, on my knees,
Consider what you're doing.  Give me heed.
Conquer your rage, renounce this bloody deed.
Spare Capulet, try without wrath to view
Him as a weak old man, condemned like you.

Let father and his daughter die in peace.
With her demise their family line will cease.
That day is not far off. Wait for that time
Do not think you will force me into crime.
I'll live for you alone, most gladly giving
To you the love of those no longer living.
I'll join you in your exile Apennine,
Willingly share your woes, make your fate mine.
With you I'll find the charms in toil and care,
Your days I'll shelter and your tears I'll share.
Your anger, Sir, appears to me to wane.
My prayers are heard; you are yourself again.
Pity's soft murmuring have reached your heart,
I have awakened Nature's healing art.

MONTAGUE:     What? I? I never ...

ROMEO:                                          Sir, cease your alarms.
Let flow your tears, open your loving arms ...

MONTAGUE:     How cruel!

ROMEO:                             Let your heart decide your fate:
For it was made to honor, not to hate.
Seek honor, nothing then on earth can hurt you.

MONTAGUE:     Leave me.

ROMEO:                             I'm yours.  I never will desert you.

ACT V

*The stage represents the tomb of the Capulets and Montagues.*

Scene 1

JULIETTE

JULIETTE:       Ye gods, with what weak strength the light of day
Into these gloomy tombs forces its way!
Beneath these crumbling vaults the ranks of those
Chained here, call me to join them in repose.
Among these shades I only take delight
In the memorial candles' flickering light.
Those tiny stars provide a small relief
From the night's horrors and my pressing grief.
Around me in the dark phantoms arise
My brother seems to float before my eyes.
And from his tomb implores me: "Do not wait;
Come rest beside me now.  Embrace your fate."
Oh God, 'tis here at last that vengeance wanes,
Where destiny gives way and virtue reigns.
Here our proud ancestors, in life by hatred driven
Embrace in death, all violence forgiven.
I come to tell them all their bitter strife
Wiped out my family and destroyed my life.
My brief unhappy life when Heaven denied
Me joy or love, I gladly cast aside.
What have I suffered?  What has been my fate?
Plotting, betrayal, suffering and hate.
Only one joy in all this dark endeavor—
Romeo's love … and he is lost forever.

Scene 2

ROMEO, JULIETTE

ROMEO:       Come quickly, we will calm her troubles yet.
'Tis said she's here …

JULIETTE:                      Who is that?

ROMEO:                                          Juliette!

JULIETTE:     Is that you, Romeo? How sweet the sight!

ROMEO:        My father's calmed, his anger put to flight.
              His heart was moved, and I have felt the charms
              Of filial love in his forgiving arms.
              You soon will see, in this retreat forlorn
              A vow of peace between our houses sworn.
              Our union he has sworn he'll not oppose.

JULIETTE:     Alas, he's not at all as you suppose.

*She gives him a letter.*

ROMEO:        What's this?  My trembling hand anticipates
              That in this note catastrophe awaits.
              Let's read:  (*He reads.*)
                          "Now is the time, devoted friends,
              When Capulet and all his family ends,
              When to the tombs I go to offer peace
              Then strike them down, and so their race will cease.
              Montague."  He cannot be kin of mine!

JULIETTE:     You see now his insidious design.
              I placed among his followers some spies
              Who traced his every move with watchful eyes.
              These faithful friends, firm in their loyalty,
              Discovering this note, brought it to me.

ROMEO:        I must prevent this bloody deed, I will ...

JULIETTE:     Remember, love, he is your father still.

ROMEO:        But he would slay you and your father too ...

JULIETTE:     I know, but there's still something we can do.

ROMEO:        Have you a plan?

JULIETTE:                      I can only save
              My country and my father from my grave.
              My house, you know, survives alone in me

As yours in you, so it is clear, you see,
If reconciliation is denied
We must remove one or the other side.
This is the only course that now remains
And so, my love, death now is in my veins.

ROMEO:     Dear God! What are you saying?

JULIETTE:                                              All is over.
Father will live, and I within my lover.
Montague will allow, thus rid of me,
Old Capulet to mourn his family,
And when he in his turn approaches death
Will let him draw in peace his final breath.
You shudder at such cruelty I see
But live on, for your country and for me.
I hear your groans, I hear and share your sighs,
But give your lover courage as she dies.

ROMEO:     Barbarous fate, would you provide me life
Yet at the cost of losing my dear wife?
At such an odious price, can you expect
That I can view the heavens with respect?
By what right do you force me to survive
Without a reason to remain alive?
Have you forgotten from our infancy
We had but one existence, you and me?
If you had truly loved me you would not
Alone the great division of death sought.
Oh dear, beloved object of my vow
Not even death should separate us now.
Let's go together, and with final sigh
Gaze on each other, with each other die.
Death, Time, and Heaven, nothing will us part
You'll live on in my soul, I in your heart.

JULIETTE:     Oh my dear Romeo, cease to reveal
For pity's sake, the passion that you feel.
Let not the memory of our passion fade,
But live, I urge you.

ROMEO:                                     No, this faithful blade
In lieu of poison will provide my rest

Despair, though tranquil, settles in my breast.
Let Montague recoil when he discovers
The dying bodies of these two cursed lovers.
My barbarous father may his deeds despise
At seeing us expire before his eyes.
I do not know why in this fatal vault
The spirit of revenge finds us at fault,
Demands our death, his lust to satisfy,
So be it then. To please him, here we'll die.

JULIETTE:      Wait, Romeo. I would not leave this life
Without becoming at the last your wife.
On the grave's brink, allow that wife to claim
You as her own, and her own husband name.
I've earned this flattering but mournful right
Our suffering hearts to join this final night.
These tombs will be our witnesses, we'll swear
Our vows upon that marble tombstone there.

ROMEO:      What are you saying?

JULIETTE:                          Farewell to this life.
I die content, my dear beloved's wife.
Give me your hand! How sweet will be my death
If in your arms I draw my final breath.

ROMEO:      She's gone! Oh barbarous father, 'twas your will
That parted us and caused us all this ill.
Yet, at the end our vows were carried through!


Scene 3

FERDINAND, MONTAGUE, CAPULET, ROMEO, JULIETTE, GUARDS, FOLLOWERS OF
FERDINAND, SUPPORTERS OF CAPULET, SUPPORTERS OF MONTAGUE, SOLDIERS,
CITIZENS

FERDINAND:      Friends, comes the moment that I promised you.
(to MONTAGUE and CAPULET)
Here, swear enmity to cease,
Revenge and hate renounce, and life in peace.
Capulet, you begin.

CAPULET:                                    I swear by those
Who rest here, this dark history will close
With me.  Friendship to Montague I give
And from this time as brothers we will live.
Our former strife forgotten, I'll respect him,
And from the slightest danger will protect him.
Come, let's embrace.  Heaven! A dagger drawn?

MONTAGUE:       Courage, my friends.

FERDINAND:                              My faithful troops press on
And separate them.

CAPULET:                          What is this?  My daughter!
Can it be possible my eyes observe such slaughter?

MONTAGUE:       Heaven is just.

CAPULET:                          Curse of my family,
Could you have wished ...

MONTAGUE:                              Her death is sweet to me.
My children are avenged.

CAPULET:                          Tiger, if you are pleased
My tears will also soothe your mind diseased.

MONTAGUE:       They will indeed.  You are as I desired.
My single heir still lives; yours has expired.

CAPULET (*showing him the body of* ROMEO):
Regard, you wretch!

MONTAGUE:                          What horror do I see!
My own dear son, cruelly ripped from me!
Is this the fruit of my inhuman rages?
Heaven, was this your will?  Are these my wages?
Here strike me down, and let me join my son.
(*He falls on the corpse of his son.*)

FERDINAND:       See what reward your cruel hate has won.
Your unjust fury led you down this path
Innocent victims falling to your wrath.

People, we will a monument erect
To give these lovers honor and respect.

# King Lear

## 1783

## Cast of Characters

Oswald

The Duke of Cornwall

Regan

Albany

Edgar

Lenox

Volwick

Kent

King Lear

Helmonde

Norclete

Strumor

Guards of Albany and Cornwall

Conspirators

# ACT I

## Scene 1

*A fortified castle belonging to the* DUKE OF CORNWALL.

THE DUKE OF CORNWALL, OSWALD

OSWALD:    My Lord, can it be here by this dark wall,
This grim construction dominating all,
The region, deep withinin the forest grim,
That I should meet with you? What was the strange whim
Caused Cornwell to remove his pleasant court
To this remote and desolate resort?

CORNWALL:    You soon shall hear, but Oswald, first relate
That news that I so eagerly await.
What word of Lear?

OSWALD:                                My Lord, for some time still
He's lingered with his daughter Volnerille.
But in his features one can clearly scan
The anger of a wounded, hurt old man
Whose thoughts still dwell upon the throne he lost.
He weeps with rage o'er what his folly cost.
When Volnerille and Albany were wed
And you her sister to the altar led,
Between you two his kingdom he divided,
And now he much regrets what he decided.
This now weighs down upon him more than age
It's even said, my Lord, that in his rage
He now regrets his treatment of Helmonde
And feels her banishment must be atoned.
He thinks her innocent and takes her side
As her two sisters grow in power and pride.
He would restore her, maybe even try
To set her sisters and their husbands by
And briefly seize again the royal crown.
The wavering old man, his fortunes down
Regrets his actions now and hopes, in vain,
To make the crown and scepter his again.

CORNWALL:     That's why I'm here. I come with the intent
              To foil that old man's restless discontent.
              I fear the thick recesses of this wood
              Hide brigands partial to old Lear, who could
              Be rallied to support his restitution.
              The English are inclined to revolution.
              Warnings of plots by Helmonde and by Lear
              Within these forests, Oswald, brought me here.
              The troops that I've brought with me I explain
              As guard against the ever-threatening Dane.
              But it's against my subjects they're deploying,
              Always, it seems, intent upon destroying
              Their betters. And they seem to understand
              Force only, so it's with a heavy hand
              I must appear, and never pity show,
              Accepting that if this means blood must flow
              That is the price required for peace to thrive.

OSWALD:       What? Do you think Helmonde is still alive?
              I've traced her steps. She's disappeared from sight.
              Her fate is swallowed up in darkest night.
              Her place of death's not certain, but it's plain
              That Volnerille and Regan fear in vain.
              Now Helmonde's earthly life is well behind her.
              Lear may dream on, but he will never find her.
              That section of his life is clearly finished,
              Though neither rage nor folly have diminished.

CORNWALL:     No, no, his fiery nature has not altered.
              He was extreme in all—he never faltered.
              In nothing did he take a middle path.
              Before his daughter suffered from his wrath,
              His other children scarcely occupied him
              And she the only gift Heaven supplied him.
              No father's love ever exceeded Lear's.
              She was his joy, the solace of his years.
              His love for her was blind as it was great,
              And it was just as strong when turned to hate.
              Kent dared to rise to her defense and he
              Was exiled for this show of sympathy.
              He's so capricious, no one ever knows
              Who next will feel his anger or his blows.
              He seems controlled for now and yet I fear

Perfidious fate has some surprises near.
Some voice within my soul a warning gives
That Helmonde is not gone, but somewhere lives.
And she could ruin all if she is living.
Oswald, do not treat lightly my misgiving.
I know my people well. Often a spark
Sets England all ablaze. Into the dark
Then. With my men, explore the forest's deeps
Search out the darkest secrets that it keeps.
Let not a crevice, not a rock slip by
The comprehensive compass of your eye.
This threatening head I urge you bring to me ...
Someone is coming! Regan, Albany,
And also Kent's two sons. Do not delay.


### Scene 2

#### CORNWALL, REGAN, ALBANY, EDGAR, LENOX

ALBANY:    Duke, duty calls me to depart today.
Our borders are established and that fact
We have confirmed by firm and mutual pact.
Negotiations finally are done,
And future enemies will find us one.
My court has long since called for my return
And I must hearken. Moreover I yearn
To see once more that wellspring of my life
The generous Lear, whose daughter is my wife.
His pomp and power gone, now wishing naught
But living in his daughter's love and thought
And dying by our side in quiet bliss.
His goodness asks for nothing more than this.

REGAN:    Duke, bear him our good wishes, say that those
Echo the ones my loving sister shows.
May he long days and sweet contentment find
And, most important, try to purge his mind
Of memories of Helmonde. He will yet grieve
Over her crimes.

LENOX:                    Her crimes! I can't believe
That she could ever do or think of ill.

CORNWALL          What, Sir, you dare suggest ...

EDGAR:                                         Brother, be still.

CORNWALL:         His father is the source of this untruth.
                  These are the thoughts of Kent ...

ALBANY:                                      Rather of youth,
                  Whose style of speaking can be rather free.
                  And yet, no crime of hers is known to me.
                  I've never tried to look into her soul;
                  Mortals should never take on Heaven's role.
                  Duchess, my Lord, I beg you to excuse me.
                  Call me again if you have need to use me.

CORNWALL:         Our powers are one, and we will not forget,
                  If once again we feel the Danish threat,
                  To join our arms to stymie their design.


## Scene 3

### CORNWALL, REGAN, EDGAR, LENOX

CORNWALL:         And you, proud scions of an ancient line,
                  Sons of brave Kent, your noble exploits make
                  A fine example for my troops to take.
                  As a reward for this, and fully earned,
                  Your father from his exile has returned.
                  Go back to him. Your valor we will miss
                  But my desire will yield to his in this.
                  Your further path your father can declare.


## Scene 4

### EDGAR, LENOX

EDGAR:            Well, brother ...

LENOX:                            I am all too well aware
                  No end is near to struggling with the Dane.

EDGAR:          And doubtless you would suffer no small pain
               If your strong arm were not in service there.

LENOX:         It would be agony, but yet I swear,
               Dear Edgar, to renounce these occupations.
               Let's go and give our father salutations
               And share his empty days. It would be wrong
               To leave him when he's been alone so long.
               His sons are all he has that he holds dear,
               And it is love for us that brought him here.
               Come now, and let those loving arms enfold you.

EDGAR:         Ye gods!

LENOX:                     Come now with me. As I have told you,
               His order was most clear.

EDGAR:                                       Our duty, too.
               His wish is sacred, that, I know, is true.
               And though in pain, alas, I must refuse.

LENOX:         Deny him?

EDGAR:                              It is not for me to choose.

LENOX:         Remember, it was he who gave us birth.
               If we stay here, there is no power on earth
               To stop him coming here, to seek us out.

EDGAR:         You think he will.

LENOX:                     He will. I have no doubt.
               So I must go to him and leave you here.
               What! Has the Count become to you so dear
               That you find nothing elsewhere to admire?
               Remember that our uncomplaining sire
               Found in his exile Nature cancelled out
               All losses. And how did this come about?
               What brought on him the wrath of unjust Lear?
               Just this—standing alone and without fear,
               He dared advise the King to keep his crown
               Bestowed by Heaven, not to cast it down,
               And yield his power which he'd not regain.

In such a court you're eager to remain?
Perhaps the poison of ambition charms you,
Whose taste conceals to what extent it harms you.
Have all our father's teachings then been lost,
Acquired at court at such a frightful cost?
His portraits of the proud manipulators,
The courtesans, the fools, the wily traitors
Hiding their evil from the monarch's eyes.
This nest of vipers, living only lies,
Scheming of new ingenious ways to hurt you,
Their vices crushing any trace of virtue,
And truth a constant sacrifice to lies.
Recall the story, with grief-stricken eyes
Of how fierce Lear, mistaken and misled,
Piled curses on his saintly daughter's head
And thrust away his once most cherished child
Disgraced, rejected, hated, and exiled,
Denouncing her, a barbarous parricide!
Later of course he never could abide
The telling of this tale; his aged eyes
Would overflow with tears ... But, why these sighs?

EDGAR:        If you but knew the scene that led to this,
If you could peer into that dark abyss,
You'd find the facts far worse than all your fears.

LENOX:        Speak, then.

EDGAR:                  Helmonde?

LENOX:                        Well, then?

EDGAR:        She was in tears.
Prince Urick, visiting our court, had grown
In love with her, and bid her share his throne.
Lear welcomed this advance with all his heart.
The joyous pair were ready to depart,
Impatient waves were trembling at the port,
A queen awaited at the Danish court,
When Volnerille, her jealous sister, sought
To foil this match and bring it all to naught.
"Beware," she said to Lear, "the power great
This marriage offers to the Danish state.

Already Norway bows to Danish lords
And Denmark can release barbaric hordes
To fall on us whenever he commands.
How then can we protect our threatened lands
If England falls into his empire now,
As marriage with my sister will allow?
He conquers us at very little cost.
Helmonde may gain a crown, but what is lost?
And have your other daughters any right?
What hope have we against proud Denmark's might?
No friend, no aid can save us from his lust.
There still is time to save us, Lord, you must
Protect us from the curse of civil war,
From bloody conflict. You must act before
An alien yoke is placed upon their necks.
Think of this union's terrible effects.
All plead with you—myself, your house, your state.
Deliver us from such a fearful fate."
Old age is weak; Lear let himself be swayed.

LENOX:    This then is why Prince Ulrick has displayed
Such anger and exhibited such force.
Lear's ill-advised rejection was the source.

EDWARD:    Yes. Ulrick left, swearing to do us ill.
Lear was in terror. Wily Volnerille
Led him to think poor Helmonde was to blame
Her pride, her coldness, only fueled this flame.
Her father's explanations she rejected,
Her sister said this was to be expected:
She blamed her father for her lover's going
Said Volnerille, and added this was owing
To wily Helmonde plotting with her mate
To upset Lear and overturn the state.
That she provided him with secret aid
And had conspired with him, arrangements made
To open England's ports unto his men.
A thousand voices rose against her then,
Calling her ingrate, traitor, even worse
The fickle public made her name a curse.
And when this turbulence at last was peaking
And seemed the theme of everybody's speaking,
The King's own ears were certainly not spared

And Volnerille, sensing his weakness, dared
To prey upon his anger and defame
Her sister. Calling down upon her name
Such crimes, that her audacity prevailed
With Lear, and absent Helmonde was assailed
As traitor, worse, as would-be parricide
Plotting to poison Lear ...

LENOX:                                          What! She implied ...

EDGAR:          She had the power. All this was believed.
And Lear, the father wounded and aggrieved,
Threw wide his doors and called on Heaven to send
Down vengeance on those plotting for his end.
"Gods, Helmonde's plot involves both me and you,"
He cried, "Let her be cast from human view.
To desolate dry valleys guide her feet
Or crush her in some mountainous retreat.
Our towns and ports to her no shelter give
No one should offer pity, while she live
And may this curse be stamped upon her features
Making her shunned by any of God's creatures
As an assassin and a parricide!"
He rose. The crowds that gathered by his side
In sympathy, drew back again in awe.
So horrible a crime one never saw.
A thousand hands bore poor Helmonde away.
I saw ...

LENOX:          No more.

EDGAR:                                          In thinking on that day
I groan now as my father often groaned.

LENOX:          Who would not weep?

EDGAR:                                          What sorrow for Helmonde!

LENOX:          Thus virtue is made wicked and obscene
And crime exalted!

EDGAR:                                          When this frightful scene
Was finished, Lear, elated and restored

Gave Volnerille unto her present Lord.
The Duke of Cornwall on that self-same day
Wed Regan, and the Dukes decided they
Would share the kingdom and become its king.

LENOX: Their rule concerns me not, the only thing
That stirs me is Helmonde. If only she
Had managed to escape this tyranny!
If only she survived her captors' might!
If her sweet eyes still opened to the light ...

EDGAR: What would you do? Speak up. Don't be afraid.

LENOX: Most eagerly I'd hasten to her aid.
Even to death, for her triumph I'd strive.

EDGAR: Lenox!

LENOX:      Edgar!

EDGAR:           My brother ...

LENOX:                She's alive!

EDGAR: Learn that this very moment ...

LENOX:                She breathes still!

EDGAR: 'Tis so.

LENOX:      Just gods!

EDGAR:                Take heart, then, if you will.
She has a champion yet, that champion, I.

LENOX: To serve her, I most willingly would die.
How did you save her?

EDGAR:                From the crowd I seized her
And covered her escape, though it displeased her
By talking of her dying far and wide.
Heaven protected us. She came to hide
Within these woods, whose craggy depths disguise

Whatever is within from curious eyes.
Only I know the way to where she hides.
Another exile harbors there, besides.
An ancient man, Morclete, has come to share
Her lonely exile.

LEXOX:                          But is she aware,
Among her woes, of Lear's unhappy fate?

EDGAR:        She is, a tale most dismal to relate.
Ungrateful Volnerille, her mate departed,
Grew ever more debased and cruel-hearted.
She taunted Lear and scorned him, till at length
She undermined his once impressive strength,
Enjoyed his sighs and undermined his pride,
Pursued unchecked this hidden parricide,
Never once troubled that the power she wielded
Had once been his and had to her been yielded.
To justify her deeds, she had reported
That Lear with certain traitors had consorted,
Stirring them up with promises that they
Would rule with him when he again held sway.
Meanwhile the court, accustomed to subjection
Accepted these base lies without objection.
I alone suffered, in my inmost being
At the profound injustice I was seeing.
Old Lear abandoned by his court and all
To Helmonde I bore witness to his fall.
Imagine, Lenox, how I strove to spare
Her ears of much I felt obliged to share.
She sat unmoving there as I was speaking
Her eyes looked out, perhaps her father seeking.
Even the unmoved gods I think would be
Aghast at such a scene of misery.
Yet Heaven seemed present, by some secret grace
Sanctity seemed to dwell within that place.
The crags, the reeds, her tears, her humble dress
In which she seemed more royal still, not less.
At times her sadness gave her brief respite,
Her lips would smile, her eyes give off a light,
Her face was bathed in tears, but one could view
Virtue and innocence shine bravely through.
Despite the ills she'd suffered and the harms,

How much her sadness added to her charms!
I urged her then to act and she agreed.
I gathered friends to help us in our need.
"My countrymen," spoke I, "a vile reign
Oppresses us. We must our rights regain.
Let rise within you your most righteous rage.
Let private wrongs with public ills engage.
You know we live in soul-destroying times
Under a reign beset with odious crimes.
Oswald, that hateful foreigner, prepares
To draw a sword upon you unawares.
That foul assassin, bounded by no ties,
Sworn to no good, and serves by craft and lies
His royal master, by whose word he's striven
To do whatever evil he was given.
And now he is among us, in this place,
And we'll soon see his crime-distorted face.
Death is his business. His the tiger's way,
And he views us as his intended prey.
Shall we go meekly to his bloody claws?
Has England ever bowed to tyrants' laws?"
I then proposed that Cornwall we should seal
In his own fortress and, that done, repeal
The laws he passed beneath which people groan
And bring deposèd Lear back to his throne.
They all agreed. I spread them out to hide
Their numbers if our movement there was spied.
Tonight their chiefs assemble at my call.
To strike the final blow. We're ready, all.
I will declare myself and lead the way.

LENOX:       And I must join you. Here I cannot stay.

EDGAR:       Our father waits. Don't you …

LENOX:                                     You know that I
             Wish only to go with you, fight and die.

EDGAR:       A noise! One comes! Great heavens, it is he!
             Our father, Kent. By no means let him see
             What we are planning; he's insist on sharing
             The fight. We must protect him from such daring.

## Scene 5

### KENT, LENOX, EDGAR

KENT:        Embrace me, children! I have feared that you
             As I have been, might be in danger too.
             I trembled lest some evil villain's snare
             Should leave the house of Kent without an heir.
             I therefore came to seek you. Your young arms
             Must now protect your father from all harms.
             The court I hate, where all conspire to hurt you.
             The wilderness is the true home of virtue.
             Come join me then in exile and be free.
             Come, dearest Edgar.

EDGAR:                          Father! (*aside*) Woe is me!

KENT:        What strange illusion makes you hesitate?

EDGAR:       Father, you know my love for you is great.
             But I cannot, and I will not explain.

KENT:        Then you come, Lenox. You, ingrate, remain.

LENOX:       I must stay too. We have some business here.

KENT:        Business? What business have you?

EDGAR:                                    Father, dear ...

KENT:        Stay, then. Your mysteries are naught to me
             And it no longer troubles me to see
             New burdens added to my aching heart.
             My sons I lose again and must depart
             To spend my final weary days alone.
             What meager blessings have the heavens shown!
             First into unjust exile was I sent
             And when, my life near end, my forces spent
             I find my sons at last, they turn aside
             And scarcely will they care when I have died.
             Dear sons, I've loved you. What was my reward?
             Tell me the business you are aiming toward?
             What insubstantial hope holds you in thrall?

(*to* EDGAR) My son, fear nothing. You can tell me all.
The project which your brother will pursue,
What is it?

LENOX:          Ah!

EDGAR:               Say nothing!

KENT:                    Tell me, true!

LENOX:          Oh, Heaven!

KENT:                Speak!

EDGAR:                     Father, my heart is breaking!
(*to* EDGAR) Consider still the risk that you are taking!

KENT:          No matter.

EDGAR:               There's much danger.

KENT:                         Let me share it.

EDGAR:          Brother, stand fast. To save him, we must bear it.
Protect our cherished father, I insist.

KENT:          No, never. I will not be so dismissed.
A noble plan can bear the light of day.
Remember your great ancestors, would they
Achieve their deeds under the cloak of night?
They fought for innocence and for the right
And won their battles in the open field.
They wanted witnesses, but here you yield
This openness. I therefore doubt your aim.
For what disturbs me, stimulates my blame,
Is why you must keep dark the plans you've made?
You are your own first victims, I'm afraid.
If you're not prey to rashness, even crime
That will bring you dishonor over time.
Why do you seek to hide them from my sight?

EDGAR:          Witness, oh Heaven, we are in the right!
Defense against your charges is denied us

But we have your own life and acts to guide us.
You unjust accusations had to bear;
We'll bear them too. We only wish to spare
Your age from perils that we see ahead.
We'll not dishonor our illustrious dead
But they will view with pride our deeds today.
And if we dare, 'twill be in such a way
Toward such a goal as well befits the brave
And you'll shed tears of joy above our grave.
Enough of death! All leads us to believe
That our endeavors will their goal achieve.
Alive and happy ...

KENT:                                    Stop! My heart is sore.
I feel my arms will ne'er embrace you more.
Farewell, cruel sons.

LENOX:                                    Yet pardon us, we pray.

KENT:     Nature demands it, and I must obey.
May Heaven, who knows your plans, your hopes fulfill.
I tremble for you both.

EDGAR:                                    I fear no ill.
Come, brother, come. I need you by my side.
Our vows, and virtue, henceforth be our guide.


Scene 6

KENT

KENT:     Alone! I'm certain Lenox would have yielded
Were not his feelings by his brother shielded.
How they resisted! Yet although they dealt
Harshly with me, still a great love I felt.
That love persists, although youth needs
To prove itself in often thoughtless deeds.
Such is the fate of fathers, though we gain
Much joy from sons, it's always mixed with pain.
For children always find a way to hurt you,
Making a burden even of their virtue!

## Scene 7

### KENT, ALBANY

ALBANY:    Count, news has come that Lear, unstable still
           Has broken with his daughter Volnerille.
           I do not know the cause, nor do I know
           Toward what part of the kingdom he may go.
           I rushed to find you and these tidings bring,
           Knowing full well your friendship with the King.

KENT:      What could have torn the two of them asunder?

ALBANY:    Some say his reason had begun to wander.
           Often this shameful weakness of the mind
           Unhappily in aged folk we find.

KENT:      Often he's felt the burden of his years.

ALBANY:    One can't postpone the natural end one fears.

KENT:      It is to be expected.

ALBANY:                              Yet Lear's fate
           Concerns us still. I beg you here to wait
           Till we have further word.

KENT:                                 Yes, I'll remain
           Until his situation is made plain.

## ACT II

### Scene 1

### KENT

KENT:        What! Lear and Volnerille abruptly parted,
And from her palace he's presumed departed.
Where can he go? Where can he make his bed?
The years weigh heavy on his snowy head.
What must he suffer as age weights him down,
His ancient brow unsheltered by a crown!
Oh, sad excess! His all too human faults
Gave rise to these calamitous results.
Yet stay! He is a father as are we;
In his mistakes our own flaws do we see.
Unhappy Lear! The blessings you bestowed
Come back as burdens to increase your load.

### Scene 2

### KENT, VOLWICK

VOLWICK:      Lord, at this moment some poor outcast waits,
Worn down by misery, outside these gates.
Seeking some shelter in their gloomy shade.
Sensing my sympathy, he sought my aid.
Telling his story, every time there came
A smile when he would light upon your name.
When I informed him that you were close by
His face lit up, a tear dropped from his eye.
He begs to see you.

KENT:                       Who is he?

VOLWICK:                     A stranger.
But one who seems to feel himself in danger.
His frozen face and hoary locks express
A long and painful story of distress.
Yet, through his tatters, one may plainly see
Clear traces of some high nobility.
In his tired eyes, now blurred by many tears,

One sees great griefs, spread over lengthy years.
He moans, "My children," and it seems quite clear
That some paternal loss has brought him here.
I read within his blushes' mute discourse
A plea for help, and so I thought, of course,
To come to you. He followed where I came
And waits in shadow, covering some shame.

KENT:    Let him appear.


### Scene 3

#### KENT, VOLWICK, LEAR

VOLWICK:    Here is the man you sought.


### Scene 4

#### KENT, LEAR

KENT (*aside*):    His eye is wandering. He sees me not.

LEAR:    Kent is not here. Now what am I to do?
He will have pity. He's a father too!
My blood! My daughter! Crowned by my own hand!
My reason falters. I can't understand!
Lear, nothing now remains, your power has flown!
Too late now to repent ... What she had shown
To me of innocence was all construction,
Designed to lure me to my own destruction.
I drove out virtue, placed crime on my throne
You only loved me, Helmonde, you alone.
I gave up all, and this is my reward!
(*looking about*) Kent is not here!

KENT (*throwing himself at* LEAR's *feet*): My Prince, my King, my Lord.

LEAR:    You recognize me, then. A friend, I see.

KENT:    My Lord, since you have deigned return to me,
Kent with you through this lifetime will remain.

LEAR:           You tear my heart.

KENT:                                    Dear Lord, your tears restrain.

LEAR:           You warned me, and I scoffed at what you said;
                Laughed at your counsels; see where this has led.
                This brow, one time ennobled by a crown,
                You see now sullied, branded, and cast down.
                Deprived of friends, of honors, all the pleasures
                The poorest agèd English subject treasures,
                I come to my last days scorned and despised
                By that proud daughter than one time I prized.
                Gods, strike cruel Vonerille with all your might!
                Her palace windows dazzle with their light.
                There festivals continue unabated;
                Her vaults are filled with symphonies created
                By court musicians, brilliant in the art
                While in the shadows, humble and apart,
                I, weeping, gnaw my pitiable crust,
                While holding back my tears, because I must.
                Indeed my pain was pleasant to her sight;
                The monster mixed her poison with delight;
                Increased her trials further to debase me,
                Encouraged crowds of mockers to disgrace me.
                Amidst their jeers I sank into despair,
                And fled the place, to find a home elsewhere.
                And yet my agonies were far from ended,
                I roamed the forests, all alone, unfriended.
                My thoughts oft turned to my rejected child;
                I searched among remote resorts and wild
                In any place she might have taken hiding.
                I felt again her sympathy abiding,
                Her charms, her virtues, and her gentle sighs,
                Her last farewell, before she quit my eyes.
                I saw her tears o'erflow, her hopes expire.
                "Father," she cried, "oh venerable sire,
                Must I become a stranger to your heart?"
                And yet I cursed her, driving us apart.
                That is the deed that weighs upon me, yet
                I still pay for it. Heaven does not forget!
                I plunged my dagger in that innocent rose.
                All of my blessings went to aid my foes
                And all my curses fell upon my friends!

O torture, agony, my arm extends
To beg you, Kent, to kill me, expiating
The life of evil I have been creating.
The wrath of gods and nature would be stilled.

KENT:        This desperate vow must never be fulfilled!
Try to endure this torment, you may find
Beyond this grief, a kind, accepting mind ...

LEAR:        Calm first the poison that corrupts my veins!
My hated daughter's image yet remains;
She dominates my thoughts. I cannot hide.
I seem to feel, within my tortured side,
A knife she turns inside me without cease.
Sometimes I seem to gain a touch of peace
When Helmonde floats again into my ken,
I near her, but she disappears again.
I tremble then with terror, blush with shame.

KENT:        Ah, do not fear her vengeance or her blame.

LEAR:        I gave her sister all; see how I'm paid.
If Volnerille such cruelty displayed,
How will Helmonde repay my crimes to her?
Her heart has hardened. She will never stir
In my behalf. Her innocence is lost,
This is my doing; I must bear the cost.
Her virtue I've destroyed by cruel force,
And I'm consumed by grief and by remorse.
And though I have been blessed at last to find
A friend in you, dear Kent. I think my mind ...
How can I say ... already is affected.

KENT:        Not so, my Lord, I wouldn't have detected ...

LEAR:        'Tis so, dear Kent. It cannot be ignored.
There is no cure for it. I fear ...

KENT:                                       What, Lord?

LEAR:        That soon or late, my reason will give way.

KENT:    Do not upon yourself such burdens lay.
         Call on the courage that has never failed you.
         Ungrateful men and women have assailed you.
         It is the fate of kings to be misled.
         Brood not on vengeance, let the gods instead
         Pursue it; leave such matters in their hands.
         Your children turn against you, seize your lands.
         But such ingratitude is not that rare
         And children's love is fleeting, so beware
         Of basing much on love which, when they're grown,
         Is turned to thoughts and pleasure of their own.

LEAR:    Dear Kent! You've suffered from your children too?

KENT:    I am a father. 'Tis what fathers do.
         What chance have we for happiness? I laid
         My trust on sons, who have this trust betrayed.
         They turn to dark conspiracies or worse
         Turning my love for them into a curse.
         If but my wife remained with me to share
         This burden. But my Lord, I'll help you bear
         Your own. Face boldly your adversity
         Together we this traitorous world will flee.
         The humble fields my ancestors endowed
         Will give us refuge from the evil crowd.
         That fertile soil will furnish our poor needs,
         With healthy grains and not with courtly weeds!
         It seeks no usury, gives up full measures,
         And our weak arms can open up its treasures.
         My heritage our simple needs will nourish.
         In my ancestral home we two can flourish.
         Accept this offer and relieve your need.

LEAR:    Dear Kent, I should ungrateful be, indeed
         If I should scorn the offer you have made me.
         But you must know, when Volnerille betrayed me
         That left my daughter Regan, who perhaps,
         Would recompense her elder sister's lapse.
         'Tis true that wounded from that other bout
         I feared a repetition, and sought out
         A hiding place till I could gather strength
         To seek out Regan. Now I have at length
         Decided my suspicions were unjust

Regan cannot, I most sincerely trust
Behave to me in such an odious way.
Her youthful years were innocent and gay
No unkind action ever did I see.
Why not trust in that happy augury?
All children can't be lacking Nature's touch.

KENT:    My Lord ...

LEAR:                    I know that Lear has suffered much,
But fortune cannot always be unjust.
Vonerille hates me now, but yet I trust
Her sister Regan will be more humane.
Forgive me, Kent. I have grown old, 'tis plain,
And old men need their children so much more
When finally they come to death's dark door.
Forgive my weakness, but I wish to see
Myself in them, at last a father be.

KENT:    My Lord, at least be careful what you do.
You have escaped one trap, don't make it two.
Be wary of another Volnerille.
I wish you well, but I am fearful still.
Don't follow my example. Be discreet.
If you have loyal friends in this retreat
I'll seek them out, their inclinations learn.
Farewell. I pray you, wait for my return,
When I can bring you news of what I find.


Scene 5

LEAR

LEAR:    No, fate has shown itself not so unkind
If it restores a friend like Kent to me.
Regan still loves her father; surely she
Will bring her mate to also take my part.
He is compassionate, with open heart.
Thanks be to God, monsters in fact are few.
Oh, Heaven, a bit of love is now my due.
In Regan's arms I will be satisfied
And if her sister Nature's laws defied

Regan will soon console me for those harms.
Daughter, I fly in rapture to your arms,
'Tis not a throne or scepter that I vie for
Quite other are the benefits I sigh for.
'Tis not a realm, but children that I seek.
I never mourned, whenever I felt weak,
The loss of rank, the empty show of state
Regan, now that my death I contemplate.
The king is gone, the father now is near.
And in that name ...


### Scene 6

LEAR, REGAN, CORNWALL, ALBANY, GUARDS OF ALBANY, *and* CORNWALL

REGAN:                              My Lord, to see you here
            Surprises us. Why? Did you fear rejection?
            You went to Kent, I'm told, an odd selection.
            Now in your arms ...

LEAR:                              My daughter, it is true
            I should have put my total faith in you!
            Embrace me, let me revel in the bliss
            Of seeing you and being loved like this!

CORNWALL:    My Lord, I see you and my spirit lifts.
            Crowned by your hands, made mighty by your gifts,
            Your friends are mine, your enemies my foes,
            Your cause is mine, so long as my blood flows.

LEAR (*to* ALBANY): Your spouse was faithful to your wishes stern
            You will not see, to darken your return
            A tiresome, aging man within your court.
            Be happy, then. I'm saddened to report
            Your wife has left you little cause for care
            Your orders have been truly followed there.
            No absent husband could have asked for more.

ALBANY:     What horror! I'm astonished and deplore
            Her action. What a monster I would be,
            Were I not grateful for your gifts to me!
            My heart belongs to you, I'll try to mend

All that my wife has ordered to offend.
With my devotion I will crush her malice
Forget the past, and come back to our palace.
I'll beg her to be gracious on my knees!

LEAR:　　　　The wrong cannot be cured by deeds like these.
Nature, your noble heart must understand.
Would be outraged, and justly, if I planned
To enter her accursed home once more.
The gods you surely know, have set great store
And weighted heavily upon their scales
All of those traits that fatherhood entails
As wisdom, power, firm authority,
All, all of which have been abused in me!
Moreover your crimes you carried out disguised,
(*to* REGAN, *mistaking her for* VOLNERILLE)
Blaming the Duke for evil you devised!
You hide those blows that you yourself confer!

REGAN:　　　You are mistaken, Lord! I am not her!
I am your Regan, not your Volnerille.

ALBANY:　　　His mind's distracted, Madam. He is ill.

REGAN:　　　These hands have never pushed away their sire.

LEAR:　　　　What! Pushed away! Do children now conspire
To push away their father in his age?
With your submissive air, can you engage
In such a crime, and try to keep it hidden?
Can such unnatural acts come forth unbidden?
Too soon I told you that you would inherit
All I possessed. What right had you? What merit?
Only your lies, perhaps the most immense
Of them against your sister's innocence,
Thus drawing down my anger on her head.
I see deceit in everything you've said,
Those showy vows, that tender sentiment,
That deep respect, I see it all was meant
To flatter me, and soon I was repaid
For my belief. I saw these honors fade
When I had given all, and I became
A burden, whose fast-flowing tears of shame

Water the thirsty earth without remark.
You thought to keep your evil in the dark
(*indicating the* DUKE OF ALBANY)
When he surprisingly brought it to view.
Yes, Duke, my pity now goes out to you
What insult to the gods gained you this spouse?
Alas I've brought dishonor to your house
And placed a threatening dagger in your bed.
How have I such a fearful monster bred?

REGAN:        You still see Volnerille in your confusion.
              Your sufferings are causing this delusion.

LEAR (*coming to himself*): Forgive me! I was unjust and unkind.
              That fury haunts me still and plagues my mind.
              My reason is still fragile, as you see.
              (*placing his hand on his heart*)
              Should it depart me wholly, it would be
              The victim of a storm my heart has made.


### Scene 7

LEAR, REGAN, CORNWALL, ALBANY, KENT, GUARDS OF CORNWALL *and* ALBANY

KENT (*aside*):    Volwick has told me all. (*to* LEAR): You are betrayed!
                   These walls cannot protect you, you will find
                   Cornwall and Regan fully as unkind
                   As Volnerille. This is a house of crime.

CORNWALL:          Put him in chains!

ALBANY:                                Wait, let us take some time.
                   We should respect his courage and his zeal.
                   What does Lear say?

LEAR:                                  To calmness I appeal.
                   I wish no civil discord to ensue.
                   (*to* ALBANY): I pity you, my friend (*to* REGAN *and* CORNWALL)
                   And as for you,
                   Unite your parricidal hands in mine.
                   (*He seizes and joins their hands.*)

|  |  |
|---|---|
| | There. All desire for vengeance I resign. |
| | Each in the other see your sire's betrayer. |
| REGAN: | What's this? |
| LEAR: | And thou, oh Nature, hear my prayer. |
| | Oh fearful nature, heed a father's plea |
| | If this inhuman pair should seek to bring |
| | A child into this world, let everything |
| | Conspire against them. If you have planned |
| | Them to be fruitful, Nature, I demand |
| | You alter this. Dry up her womb, or, better |
| | Repay her cruel conduct to the letter. |
| | Give her the sort of child that she deserves |
| | One that she idolizes but who serves |
| | Her hatefully, a son who doesn't care |
| | What he may do to drive her to despair. |
| | Who hates the age appearing in her face, |
| | Who feeds upon her shame and her disgrace. |
| | So she, consumed by tears, comes to the truth |
| | That being bitten by a serpent's tooth |
| | Causes less pain, less anguish coursing through you |
| | Than do the wrongs of people closest to you. |
| | Ungrateful children! How my heart is sore! |
| | (*to* KENT). 'Tis done, my friend. I am a father no more. |
| REGAN: | My Lord! |
| LEAR: | Begone! |
| ALBANY: | My Lord! |
| LEAR: | Begone! |
| ALBANY: | What hate! |
| CORNWALL: | Duke, we must pacify his furious state! |
| LEAR: | Ingrates, farewell, and take with you my curse. |

Scene 8

LEAR, KENT

LEAR:    Dear friend, your arm. My state is getting worse.
KENT:    This last misfortune was the worst I know.

LEAR:    You pity me?

KENT:    Alas!

LEAR:    Then let us go.
This life of mine is but a fragile thing.
You hear my groans?

Scene 9

KENT, LEAR, VOLWICK

KENT:    What tidings do you bring?

VOLWICK:    My tears reveal my message. As you fear
The barbarism of this house is clear.
This palace we must flee now, without fail.

KENT:    What! Now! At night!

VOLWICK:    Yes, though a fearful gale
The worst e'er seen, awaits us with its wrath,
Threatening doom to all within its path.

KENT:    At night!

VOLWICK:    Go now, and bear the king away.

KENT:    I will.

VOLWICK:    Prison awaits you if you stay.

LEAR:    I go to greet with pleasure wind and rains.
The lightning flashes. Will you share my pains?
KENT:    My Lord, my life is yours, while life remains.

## ACT III

## Scene 1

### EDGAR, LENOX, CONSPIRATORS

*A forest bristling with rocks; in the rear a cavern near an ancient oak. It is night. A furious storm is rising.*

EDGAR (*to the* CONSPIRATORS): My brother Lenox, like you warriors, longs
To lend his strength to right our country's wrongs.
To me he's joined by blood and unto you
By honor, and to both he shall be true.
As I have warned you, Oswald now is here.
He joined his master Cornwall and it's clear
He and the tyrant have some secret plan
To cause us all much suffering, if they can.
Much more surprising, Cornwall brags
That he will seek us out among these crags,
And ferret out our well-disguised retreats.
Friends, we must march at once. The war drum beats.
Our righteous anger who will dare oppose?
We'll save the nation and defeat its foes,
Replace a wronged king upon his throne,
Reject his children, bid him reign alone.

CONSPIRATOR:   As King and father both his loss is great.

EDGAR:   One can but weep at his tormented state.

CONSPIRATOR:   Helmonde is well revenged.

EDGAR:                                                    Yet she was first
To weep when Lear's misfortunes on him burst.
'Tis time, my friends, this secret was revealed
Within these woods Helmonde I've kept concealed
An old man guards her, who is not aware
Of what a prize I've placed within his care.
I've kept this secret so your motivation
Would only be to help our suffering nation.
But her sad state has formed in me, I own
A strong desire to see her on the throne.
It is my vow to her that guides my actions,

> To gather patriots from many factions,
> To join together in a common cause,
> To doom the tyrants and restore the laws.
> Heaven, the night, the forest give us cheer.
> We fight for whom? For Helmonde and for Lear.
> Each one of you has born these tyrants' cost;
> Possessions taken, family members lost.
> Ye gods, remember Lear and let us be
> The arms that bring his back to sovereignty.
> Our hearts are free, and in your cause we rose
> Use us to be your force against your foes!
> They have rejected beauty, age, and you.
> Our swords are ready; give to them their due!
> And if we die, may jealous fathers place
> Upon our tombs: "They glorified our race."

CONSPIRATOR: Friends, let us join our hands, our friendship seal.

EDGAR:     Cease now these vows, these statements of your zeal.
Another merits them and she is near,
The good Helmonde, and she will soon appear.
I go this instant to present her to you.

*He enters the cavern.*


## Scene 2

### LENOX, CONSPIRATORS

LENOX (*seeing* HELMONDE): Virtuous lady, what delight to view you!
Heaven and earth have destined you for power.


## Scene 3

### LENOX, EDGAR, HELMONDE, CONSPIRATORS

EDGAR:     'Tis she whose cause has gathered us this hour.
May this abode that sheltered her be blessed;
She wept for Lear here; Heaven did the rest.

HELMONDE: You souls compassionate, the gods are just.
They'll bless your projects. In this hope I trust.
They know the ills my heart has felt are great,
But wounded still, it has not sheltered hate.
My father's tears have been my chief concern.
Ingrates in power to oppression turn.
Heav'n made you English, therefore you rebel.
With mingled prayers and tears I wish you well.
Restore my father, now so beaten down
With shame, and place upon his brow his crown.
Above all, let him find me without blame.
But if the gods had spared us all the shame
Of these tyrannic rulers, I have rather
Sheltered my father from this bitter weather
Even in this remote and cheerless place
To offer humble solitude and grace,
Comfort his age, protect him from all harms,
And bid him lose his troubles in my arms.

EDGAR: We recognize again our Helmonde now.
And Madam, we extend to you our vow.
First, by my sword, which I to you extend ...
(*thunder and lightning*)

CONSPIRATOR: Heavens! What lightning! What does this portend?

LENOX: What's this? A sign that Heaven itself has sent?

EDGAR: It bids us to avenge the innocent.
Swear all to bring again Lear's sovereignty,
Die for Helmonde, or conquer all with me!
(*All draw their swords.*)

CONSPIRATORS: We swear!

EDGAR: My friends, this is a fearful night
With fire the very heavens are alight,
And thunder roars around us where we stand.
Yet each man has his weapon in his hand.
March on! But in our righteous wrath must we
Spare from our blows the Duke of Albany.
Respect his virtue. Lenox, lead the way.
Speed is essential. I, without delay

Will bring more troops to join us, standing by
And we together shall prevail or die.

LENOX *and the* CONSPIRATORS *leave.*


Scene 4

HELMONDE, EDGAR

HELMONDE:     Ah, will you leave me?

EDGAR:                                            I cannot delay.
It is the call of honor I obey.

HELMONDE:     The peril is great.

EDGAR:                                            That pleases me the more.

HELMONDE:     This peaceful stream, alas, shall flow with gore!
All your brave friends ...

EDGAR:                                            Their fate they will embrace,
Knowing it is for you their death they face.
Soon Lear, avenged by their heroic blood ...
Ye gods! You weep!

HELMONDE:                                  Rumors have reached the wood
That my unhappy father has departed
From Volnerille's dominions, broken-hearted.

EDGAR (*aside*):   Ah, Heaven! (*to* HELMONDE) Trust not what idle tongues have
said.

HELMONDE:     Who knows where the abused old man has bled,
If he still lives, for Regan, I've heard tell
Has pitilessly banished him as well.
(*great noise of thunder and lightning*)
If such as been his fate, ye storms severe,
Fall not upon the head of homeless Lear!
Ye gods, remember that while he still reigned,
He kept your dictates and your laws maintained.
Do not upon his head your lightning cast

Divert from him Boreas's icy blast!
Let him not feel the icy tempest's pain.
I do not ask you to restore his reign,
Only preserve his life, his wandering feet
Guide to his daughter in reunion sweet.
If I might clasp him once more in these arms
He could forget his other daughters' harms!
I'd die of pleasure, seeing him once more.

*Great burst of thunder and lightning.*

EDGAR:          The very heavens seem convulsed in war;
                The silent earth lies trembling now in fear.

HELMONDE:       At least, dear Edgar, you are staying near.
                Ah, do not leave me.

EDGAR:                                    Peace. There is no doubt
                These humble walls will keep the tempest out.
                In sanctuary here you may abide
                Leaving the storm's cruel punishments outside.
                Your heavenly eyes will not reflect its fire.

HELMONDE:       I tremble, Edgar.

EDGAR:                          Madam, come, retire.
                Though storms may rage, though earth from Heaven may
                Part,
                The gods will yet protect the pure in heart.

*They enter the cave.*

## Scene 5

### LEAR

LEAR:           The winds increase. I have lost sight of Kent.
                My steps are wandering and my strength is spent.
                In vain I search ... and in the darkness see
                Only dark forces bent on crushing me.
                (*Thunder, lightning, wind. Hail falls on* LEAR's *unprotected
                head.*)

Heaven, increase your blows, by fury fed,
Let fall your fires, your tempests on my head!
I'll not complain, release on me your might;
Show Lear no mercy, he gives up that right.
Let loose your anger while he still endures,
This dying body, this old head are yours.
This forehead, sheltered by a few white hairs,
Which neither wind nor driving tempest spares,
Forget that these thin locks once bore a crown.
By my own hand my house has tumbled down.
I therefore take your blows, devoid of pride,
Abandoned in these woods without a guide.
Torn from the tender friend who shared my grief,
Chilled by your winds, alone upon the heath,
Driven from home, a figure of dejection,
His reason tottering from his rejection.


Scene 6

LEAR, KENT

KENT (*appearing from the trees*): My Prince!

LEAR:                                        Dear Count!

KENT:          At last your steps I've traced.

LEAR:                                     We are united.

KENT (*aside*):    Ah, what trials he's faced!
                   (*to* LEAR): I called you, but it seems you were distraught.

LEAR:          Kent, think of all those poor souls who were caught
               Out in this storm, and bless the innocent
               Who slept in peace although the skies were rent.
               But those within the palace over there.
               May the gods strike them down, and nothing spare
               To punish them. Speak, in the thunder's roar
               Did you not hear the doom they have in store?
               Then let them tremble, in this fearful time.
               I am at peace, for I have done no crime.
               I have been sinned against, but done no sin.

KENT:   The storm still rages, we must go within.
        You tremble with the cold ...

LEAR:                               Dear friend, you see,
        From Nature's rage not even kings are free.

KENT:   I know this from the hardships you endure.

LEAR:   But grief has taught me pity for the poor.
        Alas, the king, upon his lofty height
        Feels all too weakly his poor subjects' plight.
        Some old man may be dying as we speak.
        Unknown to us, how many poor folk seek
        Some small relief, far distant from our care.
        Doubtless I've overlooked the pain they bear.

KENT:   No, no, your people never cried in vain.

LEAR:   Do you believe that I still feel their pain?

KENT:   They're not ungrateful.

LEAR:                           Yet my children are.

KENT:   Their names from my lips I will henceforth bar.
        (*Lightning illuminates the mouth of the cavern.*)
        'Tis late, we must away ... the storm revealed
        A shelter which was hitherto concealed.
        Do you not see it?

LEAR:                       No, I nothing spied.

KENT:   Follow my steps; I'll lead you safe inside.

LEAR:   You wish it?

KENT:                Let us go.

LEAR:                           Dear Count, hold back!

KENT:   Do not allow this storm a fresh attack;
        What grim foreboding will not let you rest?

LEAR:            A troubled spirit rages in my breast.

KENT:            My Lord, my sovereign master, hear my prayer.
                 Heaven perhaps will pity your despair.
                 Do not resist me; in these woods tonight
                 The wildest beast has hidden away in fright.
                 Yet you alone, who once were great indeed
                 Cannot accept the shelter that you need.
                 Lord, let us enter here, our last resort.
                 I will be all to you—friends, children, court.
                 Your sufferings are mine, your pain I feel.
                 Must my tears flow to prove to you my zeal?
                 Before your honored knees I'll kneel and pray ...

LEAR:            You break my heart.


                        Scene 7

                 LEAR, KENT, NORCLETE

NORCLETE:        Who's there?

KENT:                        Two souls, astray.
                 Seeking a shelter on this savage night.

NORCLETE:        My humble cave is yours; I share your plight.
                 Someone would harm you?

LEAR:                                    More than I can bear.
                 One finds ungrateful children everywhere.

NORCLETE:        For many families that indeed holds true.

LEAR:            You gave all to your daughters too?

NORCLETE:        Not all. This humble shelter still to me is left.

LEAR:            Your children then did not leave you bereft?

NORCLETE:        Death has long since removed them from Norclete.

LEAR:            You are still happy; you have your retreat.

NORCLETE (*aside*): His fate fills me with pity.

LEAR:                                          Know you why?
              The wind so roars, and lightning fires the sky?
              Why distant mountain peaks erupt in flame?

NORCLETE:     No. Why?

LEAR (*mysteriously*): My fearful crime. I am to blame.
              Friend! You draw back! Wait! I make no complaint.

NORCLETE:     What have you done?

LEAR:                                 My daughter, free of taint ...
              (*Suddenly his face brightens at the distant memory.*)
              Yes, I remember. She was young and fair.

*He falls into a reverie.*

KENT:         He does not hear us.

NORCLETE:                         Have you lost her? Where?

KENT:         Alas, we know not.

NORCLETE:                         And was she alone?

KENT:         Why do you ask, old man? Is something known?

NORCLETE:     The darkness of that cavern hides from view
              A maiden, virtuous, but secret too.

KENT:         Who is she? Speak!

NORCLETE:                           I only know that she
              Without hope of reward, takes care of me.

KENT:         Her birth?

NORCLETE:                     Her dress suggests, as do her ways,
              That in this forest she has spent her days.

KENT:         Do you suspect her heart may secrets bear?

NORCLETE:    Indeed, some torment may be hidden there.
             Sometimes she moans, "My father, give him peace!"

KENT:        So be it, Heaven! May his troubles cease.
             (to NORCLETE)
             Who brought her to you?

NORCLETE:                              A young man.

KENT:                                            His name?

NORCLETE:    Edgar.

KENT:                    My son! Wake, Lear! Your reason claim!
             Ye gods, come to his aid. My King, prepare
             To find new hope and joy.


## Scene 8

### LEAR, KENT, NORCLETE, HELMONDE, EDGAR

KENT (*continuing*): Look, they are there!

HELMONDE:                          Oh joy!

KENT:                                My son!

EDGAR:                                     My father!

KENT:        Edgar, dear,
             Approach your loving father without fear.
             Your care preserved me. Heaven be praised and see,
             Here is your prince.

HELMONDE:                          My father! Is it he?

KENT:        My King, your daughter. Come to yourself and greet
             That precious being now kneeling at your feet.

LEAR (*vacantly*): Of whom speak you?

KENT:                                    Of someone you must cherish
                   Who weeps for you, and will not let you perish.
                   Your daughter.

LEAR (*pushing her away in horror*): Heavens!

HELMONDE:                                    Ah, he knows me not.

LEAR:              Our enemies have found us. We are caught!
                   (*to* HELMONDE): Know you my name?

HELMONDE:        'Tis Lear.

LEAR:                          And yours?

HELMONDE:                                    Your child.

LEAR:              Seize her! 'Tis Volnerille, that monster wild,
                   Or evil Regan. Do you recognize
                   The one who gave you all, whom you despise.
                   By your advice his love for Helmonde vanished
                   By your intrigues that innocent was banished.
                   Now vengeance ...

HELMONDE:                          Hold!

LEAR:                                 No mercy!

HELMONDE:                                              I entreat ...

LEAR (*seizing her*): I'll drag you to the heavenly judgment seat
                   Where the gods wait, and their high court decides ...

KENT:              Forget, if possible, those parricides.


LEAR:              What, I forget! Ye gods, I here implore you.
                   The trembling accused stand now before you.
                   I here affirm these children so unkind
                   These cruel ones were always in my mind.
                   You should have given murderous children to them
                   So that at last like me they'd come to rue them.
                   The time has come to crush them, do not fear

That any blood of theirs will interfere.
Hurl down your judgment. Give me satisfaction.
I'll sit beside you and applaud your action.

KENT:          Pity sometimes leads us to clemency.

LEAR:          The love of vengeance was not born in me.

HELMONDE (*to* KENT): May I speak with him?

KENT:                              Shortly. It appears
His o'ercharged heart needs this release of tears.
I pray you, let them flow.

LEAR:                              My Volnerille,
My Regan, daughters, why do you use me ill?
Did you not feel that anything was due
For those great benefits I gave to you?
Are you devoid of Nature's noblest feature
That seeks the good in every living creature?
The youthful vulture, in his lofty nest
Sinks not his tooth into his mother's breast:
Yet you have driven your father from your door
And into exile, desolate and poor!
I had a throne, alas! 'Twas given to you;
'Twas done in love. What punishment is due?

KENT:          You weep!

LEAR:                              I feel my wound. Indeed I weep.
Condemned to wander in these forests deep.
No aid! No shelter! By my sorrows driven,
Gods! Take away the heart I have been given!
(*His expression and voice change.*)
I will no longer weep.

HELMONDE:                              His features change.

KENT:          He suffers from the storm, and from these strange
Events. His torment is not near its end.

HELMONDE:          We all must gather to support him, friend.

LEAR (*to* NORCLETE): Old man, approach.
            (*to* KENT): You, friend, with your firm hand
            Hold back these furies. Give them your command.

HELMONDE:     How his heart trembles!

KENT:                       He is sore distressed!

LEAR:         Dear friends, pull off these serpents from my breast!
            Gods, I am dying!

HELMONDE:                What great pain he bears!

LEAR:        See, at my gaping wounds their sharp tooth tears!
            See how my blood pours down, my flesh is rent!

HELMONDE:     These snakes his cruel children represent.

LEAR:        Ungrateful!

HELMONDE:            Friends, he's fainting. Give him air.
            Gods, reunite us. Gods, my tomb prepare!

LEAR:        What do I hear?

HELMONDE:          My grief.

LEAR:                    Your looks are kind.
            Near you, I feel a soothing in my mind.
            She was your age.

HELMONDE:             But if the gods again
            Restored her to your arms ...

LEAR:                  That is my pain—
            I dare not hope ...
HELMONDE:             But should she now appear,
            Seek your embrace, would she be welcome here?

LEAR:        What's that? My victim see for this last time?

HELMONDE:     Would you no longer love her?

LEAR:                                          For my crime
                 With my own sword I would put out my eyes.

HELMONDE:        But could it be her love for you you prize
                 No longer ...

LEAR:                            See my misery! I fear
                 My reason is perhaps no longer clear.
                 I tremble, I don't know if I should heed
                 That sweet presentiment that I so need.
                 It brings a calm to fancies dark and wild.
                 Some instinct tells me that you are my child.
                 But it may be, my agony to ease,
                 Your noble spirit seeks my heart to please ...
                 Are you my blood?

HELMONDE:                          My father!

LEAR:                                          Farewell, fears!

HELMONDE:        Helmonde is in your arms! Let flow your tears!

LEAR (*drawing his sword and offering to wound himself*):
                 Since you are here, this is my just reward!

HELMONDE:        Gods, what is this?

LEAR:                                     Your vengeance!

HELMONDE:                                     Hold, my Lord!
                 I have misled you. Helmonde is not here.

LEAR:            You stole a virtuous name all must revere!
                 Go, fly my sight, inflict no further pain.
                 Helmonde, alas, is gone—the heavens remain,
                 Those heavens to whose fierce rage I've bared my head,
                 Resume your tempests, come now, strike me dead!
                 Ah cruel heavens, could you drive away
                 That virtuous soul, however she might pray?
                 (*Raises his arms to Heaven.*)
                 My daughter, see my grief, beyond all measure.
                 Can my great suffering give you any pleasure?
                 Your sisters have condemned me for my crime.

Now, dying, I call on you one last time.
Pardon this old man, torn by his remorse,
He perishes, a broken heart the source.
Have pity on him, gods.

EDGAR:                                    Helmonde!

KENT:                                                        My King!

HELMONDE:    Look to my father, Edgar. Can we bring
No peace to him? Alas, dear friends, I see
No end to pain for him or life for me.
Oh Heaven, bring this tortured soul relief
And benefits to recompense his grief!

*They carry the unmoving* LEAR *into the depths of the cavern.*

ACT IV

Scene 1

*Same setting as* ACT III. KENT, EDGAR

KENT:           Edgar, your courage and your zeal are bound
                In the most worthy cause you could have found.
                I heartily approve your generous deeds
                In aid of those who have the greatest needs.
                But say, where is your brother?

EDGAR:                                      He will bring
                The forces needed to avenge our king.
                But time is precious. Prudence now demands
                We place both sire and daughter in their hands.
                I know the paths, and I will lead the way
                To bring them to the camp without delay.
                What spirit it will give our troops to see
                These noble souls with them again and free.
                At last it seems that we will win the game,
                Gathered as one in Nature's holy name.
                An old man leads us, his misfortunes great
                As are his years, yet he will head our state.
                The gods themselves will make our weapons strong
                Committed as they are to right his wrong.
                How soon can we be ready and away?

KENT:           But who will guide his steps after this day?
                How can the crown be placed upon his brow
                When he cannot command his reason now?
                Will he not shame the state that he was born
                To rule, a thing of pity and of scorn?

EDGAR:          Do not despair. In his tormented breast
                Recent events have brought a certain rest.
                The sweetness of repose, its soothing charms
                Have been a balm to temper his alarms.
                A soothing sleep now spreads throughout his veins
                Forgetfulness and soothing of his pains.
                His all-consuming rage has run its course.
                Soon all will disappear, except remorse,
                And may rekindle that celestial fire

His children's cruelty caused to expire.
His mind's confusion was not caused by age.
Another sort of blow induced his rage;
A deep and cruel pain has torn apart
A father's generous and trusting heart.
But if I'm not deceived, now we can trace
Some happiness and peace upon his face.

## Scene 2

### KENT, EDGAR, HELMONDE

HELMONDE:    Dear Count, after the storms that we have suffered
The angry gods, it seems, their rage has buffered.
Daylight returns and with it our hopes rise
That love will shower on us from these skies.
Not just for us, I pray its gentle light
Will fall upon my father's troubled sight!
If his dear eye, so long with tears aflow
My now be healed by this celestial glow.
And now, his suffering past, his sins atoned
May he descry at last the dear Helmonde!
But if these dearest hopes I hold in vain
Console me friends, and help me bear my pain.

EDGAR:    Enough, dear Madame. I will find Norclete;
The dream you have may find fulfillment yet.

*He leaves.*

## Scene 3

### KENT, HELMONDE

KENT:    Madame, forgive and pardon my son's haste
His men await, their trust he cannot waste.
He'll soon return, meanwhile you will be guided
To join those faithful who with you have sided.

## Scene 4

### KENT, HELMONDE, LEAR, EDGAR, NORCLETE

EDGAR *and* NORCLETE *enter bearing* LEAR *on a bed of roses and place him facing the rays of the rising dawn entering the cavern.*

KENT (*to* HELMONDE): Madame, your father.

HELMONDE:                                                   Heaven!

EDGAR (*to* HELMONDE):                                        Will you allow
        Me to take arms defending your cause now?
        (*to* NORCLETE):
        You know our plans. To your retreat keep near
        Whatever happens you will see and hear.
        Suspect whatever happens in this wood,
        Its darkness masks the ill as well as good.
        The faintest noise, a voice, a footfall light
        Report at once to us, however slight.

NORCLETE:     I'll eagerly perform whatever task
        You give me, Sir. You only have to ask.

*He leaves with* EDGAR.

## Scene 5

### KENT, HELMONDE, LEAR

HELMONDE:     What think you, Count, now, of my father's state?
        Can we now hope his troubles will abate?
        Does his calm visage promise him relief?

KENT:         I see there nothing that should bring you grief.

HELMONDE (*softly kissing the sleeping* LEAR's *face*):
        Dear father, may my mouth bring peace
        Unto your troubled heart, and sweet release!
        Under my tender care may you be cured
        Of all the wounds and blows you have endured.

KENT (*aside*):    What virtue, Heaven. How could any choose
To darken you with false, malicious hues!

HELMONDE:    How could my sisters whom to you both owe
Their lives, refuse to heed your cries of woe?
(*weeping*) Father, did you deserve to be outcast
To bend your head before the tempest's blast?
Alas, I've seen this brow, these whitened locks
Glow in the lightning, feel the wind's rude shock.
I would on such a night, such horrors seeing
Give shelter to the humblest human being;
Yet you my father, must contented be
With that small aid that Heaven has given me—
These loving arms, this cave where we abide
The scorn of men, allowing us to hide,
This humble cot, covered in softening reeds
Are what has been accorded for your needs.
Ah! If your griefs have made your mind unstable
I will serve you as long as I am able.
(*to* KENT):
His wandering reason, can it be repaired?

KENT:    There are some plants from which can be prepared
A soothing draft which many have opined
Has power to restore a wandering mind.

HELMONDE:    Oh precious plants the gods have made to buffer
The fearful ills that human beings may suffer,
If you can hear me, tears of mine may nourish
Your healing powers. May you grow and flourish
To heal my father, and may soothing sleep
Its faithful watch over this healing keep.
From my own sorrows grant me no release
Till you have brought my suffering father peace.
Ah, Count, his face is lightening. Look there!

KENT:    Heaven has surely heard your pious prayer!

HELMONDE:    His wandering reason yet he may regain.
His features show a rising calm again.
He wakens.

LEAR:                              Gods, why do you lift my gloom?
          Why have you forced me to depart my tomb?
          (*charmed by the rays of the rising sun*)
          This gentle light but adds to my confusion;
          This dawn, this place, it all seems an illusion
          My wandering eye but vaguely understands.
          I scarcely dare lift up my trembling hands.
          I pity my condition, feel my shame.

HELMONDE:    Look at me, Lord, I love you all the same.

LEAR:        Ah, lady, mock me not.

*He moves to put himself at HELMONDE's feet.*

HELMONDE:                        Arise, Sir, please!
          It's I who should be falling at your knees.

LEAR:        You see, I'm weak.

HELMONDE:                      Alas!

LEAR:                                My end is near.
          Upon my head is piled up many a year.
          Save me.

HELMONDE:          From whom?

LEAR:                            From those who ... But, it seems,
          That you know nothing of their plots and schemes.

HELMONDE:    Who are these enemies?

LEAR:                          My wits are weak.
          My memory fades.

HELMONDE:                    And yet some folk still speak
          Of your past glory.

LEAR:                          True. This arm you see
          Has led the way to many a victory.

HELMONDE:    Under what banner? Were you perhaps a king?

LEAR:          No, but a father, a far nobler thing.

HELMONDE:      Unhappy fathers weigh on you, I'd guess.

LEAR:          I've always thought on them and their distress.
               The name of father has for me great charm.

HELDEMONDE:    Alas, I know one who has known much harm.

LEAR:          Your own?

HELMONDE:                      O God!

LEAR:                               You weep for him?

HELDEMONDE:                                      I do.

LEAR:          You love him? Why is he not here with you?
               Is he alive? And is his dwelling near?

HELMONDE:      He lives.

LEAR:                  What is his name?

HRLMONDE:                               His name is Lear.

LEAR:          I know him not.

HELMONDE:                  Alas!

LEAR:                          Does he know you?

HELMONDE:      Not he.

LEAR:                  Why not?

HELMONDE:                              His troubles overthrew
               His reason.

LEAR:                          Ah, what was the cause of such
               Distress?

HELMONDE:                                His children, whom he loved too much.

LEAR:                    Children all seem to suffer from ingratitude,
                         But you, my dear, seem not to share this attitude.
                         You love the gods, and feel you father's worth?

HELMONDE:                I've had no greater gift upon this earth.

LEAR:                    Ah, if the gods had given me such a child!
                         But, no ...

HELMONDE:                                Go on.

LEAR:                                         They gave me furies wild
                         Who in their wrath ...

HELDEMONDE:                             Who were they?

LEAR:                                                   I still see
                         Their angry faces.

HELMONDE:                               What atrocity
                         Did they commit? Think. What was it about?

LEAR:                    A palace ... night ... a storm ... they cast me out.

HELMONDE:                What were their names? Do you recall them still?

LEAR:                    Regan was one.

HELMONDE:                              The other?

LEAR:                                            Volnerille.

HELMONDE (*indicating* KENT): These warrior features do you recognize?

LEAR:                    It is my old friend Kent, I realize.
                         (*to* HELMONDE, *slowly overcoming his confusion*):
                         But you?

HELMONDE:                Alas, I am no stranger, as you thought.

LEAR:                    You said you had a father whom you sought.

HELMONDE: I did.

LEAR:       Still living, but whose sorrows were great.
You love him?

HELMONDE:     Without doubt.

LEAR:          Ah cruel fate
That separated you! Now, my mind is clearing.
Have you two sisters?

HELMONDE:        Heaven be praised for hearing
My prayers. He's healing. We are truly blessed.

LEAR: My hearts is trembling, bounding in my breast.
Yes, you have sisters. And I now recall
I gave my throne ... my rising spirits fall.
My reason fails. Gods, stabilize my light
Or plunge me living in the tomb's dark night!
(*to* HELMONDE): What should I say to you? Instruct me, pray.
My mind restored, I know not what to say.
Whoever you may be, give me your aid.
Do not desert me!

HELMONDE:       Ah, I am afraid ...

LEAR: Your tears, I know, some mystery conceal.
Your name, your father, please, you must reveal!
Sweet hope! Great gods, let this be no mistake!
Reason return, and happiness awake!
(*to* KENT)
My friend, I feel I'll die of happiness.

KENT (*low to* HELMONDE): I fear his heart will not survive the stress.

HELDEMONDE: My arms reach out, clearly the strength I lack
To still resist.

LEAR:     My heart cries out!

KENT:         Hold back.

HELMONDE: Nature insists.

LEAR:                                My blood makes matters clear.

HELMONDE:    I am Helmonde.

LEAR:                          My daughter!

HELMONDE:                                          Father dear!
We are united now; our woes are done.
Our destinies, our souls, our tears are one.

LEAR:        My daughter's tears pour balm upon my heart
And cure my wounds by Nature's healing art.
They bring relief to bloody wounds still fresh.
Ungrateful children tore into my flesh.
I feel upon my face your soft tears pouring
Calming my soul, my wandering mind restoring.
Your gentle touch, the warmth of your embrace
Full centuries of torments would erase.
Ye gods if one last wish I might express
I'd die, a father, in this happiness.

HELMONDE:    My most profound desire has now come true
To live and die for you and next to you.

LEAR:        Daughter, what trials have you had to face?

HELMONDE:    My Lord, let me conduct you from this place.
The tyrants hate you, but your friends are nigh.
Edgar has shrewdly hidden them nearby.
He soon will come to join us with those friends.
And thus the bloody reign of traitors ends.
Your crown will be restored as is your due.

LEAR:        To be passed on, my daughter, unto you.
Oh noble Edgar!

KENT:                          In him you can trust.

LEAR:        You blood is his. Your confidence is just.

HELMONDE:    He guarded me in my adversity.

LEAR (*to* KENT):   As you, dear friend, in mine watched over me.
You will avenge Lear and his dearest child.


## Scene 6

### KENT, HELMONDE, LEAR, NORCLETE

NORCLETE:   Madame, while roaming through this forest wild,
I chanced upon a soldier who revealed
That Regan's men have taken to the field
To counter Edgar, and these woods so quiet
Will soon resound with armed clash and riot.
He thinks this conflict will inspire the folk
To turn against the Dukes, throw off their yoke
Drive them from power, heap them with disgrace
And bring back Lear to rule us in their place.
I hastened to return, but drawing near
I made a discovery to cause you fear.
Among the rocks and trees I chanced to spy
The soldiers of the Duke and quite nearby
Their cautious movements and attentive air
Left little doubt what they were doing there.
They certainly are seeking to surprise you.

HELMONDE (*to* LEAR): I pray you, Lord, allow me to advise you.
I fear for you. I, under this disguise
Can easily escape their searching eyes.
Alas, you are the one that we must save
Hide in the deep recesses of this cave.

LEAR:   What, hide!

KENT (*pointing out* HELMONDE *to* LEAR):
Ah, Lord, regard your daughter's fear.

LEAR (*following* HELMONDE): I'll trust in you, my daughter, keep me near.

*He goes into the cavern depths with* HELMONDE.

## Scene 7

### KENT, NORCLETE

KENT:     Ye gods, who human battles watch and weigh
          See Lear and Cornwall as they meet today!
          Their different causes you appreciate.
          The parties meet; you must decide their fate.
          The honor of this fight I must forego
          But let my sons avenge my master's woe.
          The posts of greatest danger let them take
          And by their glory reputations make.
          If they cannot alive return to me,
          Then let their dear blood purchase victory.
          You'll hear from Kent no reprimand, no sigh,
          If for their King's deliverance they must die.

## Scene 8

### KENT, NORCLETE, HELMONDE

HELMONDE:  I breathe again, dear Kent, for we have found
           Nearby, an ancient oak which near the ground
           Conceals a hollow. There my father lies
           Safely concealed from any searching eyes.

## Scene 9

### KENT, NORCLETE, HELMONDE, OSWALD, SOLDIERS

OSWALD:     Whose home is this?

NORCLETE:                           Mine.

OSWALD:                                  And your name?

NORCLETE:                                               Norclete.

OSWALD (*pointing to* KENT): And who is this?

NORCLETE:                                    A guest whom I have let
     Reside a while, he having asked of me
     The natural rights of hospitality.

OSWALD (*pointing to* HELMONDE):
     And she?

NORCLETE:                           My daughter.

OSWALD:                                      Rumors now abound
     That in these woods a traitor may be found.

HELMONDE:    What traitor?

OSWALD:                          Lear.

HELMONDE:                                 The sorrows he endured
     Surely by now his passing have assured.

OSWALD:    News of his passing, then, has come to you?

HELMONDE:    So it is said. I hold it to be true.

OSWALD (*to his* SOLDIERS):
     Men, to your duty. Take up torches. See
     Who's hiding in this cave's obscurity.

*The* SOLDIERS *light their torches and a lantern which lluminates the cave.*
OSWALD *descends with them into the cave and they look into all its passages.*

HELMONDE (*trembling, in a low voice, to* KENT):
     I fear they'll find whatever we're concealing.

KENT (*also in a low voice*): Don't let them see the anguish you are feeling.

HELMONDE:    Gods, hear us.

NORCLETE:                          Though I try to hide my fear.
     My blood runs cold at feeling them so near.

OSWALD (*to his soldiers*): Lear is not here. Move on.
     (*to* NORCLETE): And you, old man,
     If Lear seeks shelter here, his presence ban.

> He may come trembling, consumed with fright
> And beg you give him shelter for the night.
> Turn a deaf ear, and leave him to his fate.

HELMONDE:    Is he then menaced with a peril so great!

OSWALD:    If Cornwall or his men should flush him out ...

HELMONDE:    What would his fate be?

OSWALD:                                Death, without a doubt.

HELMONDE *falls fainting into the arms of* NORCLETE.

OSWALD (*regarding* HELMONDE):
> She swoons. There's something hidden from our view.
> Arrest her.

KENT (*drawing his sword*): Hold!

OSWALD:                        Stranger, what would you do?

KENT:    Defend her though alone.

OSWALD:                                    A vain display.
> Soldiers, bind up his hands, without delay.

KENT:    Cruel monster, do you dare ...

OSWALD:                                Bind him, I said.

KENT:    You'll bind me only after I am dead.
> And I will render you such harm before ...


Scene 10

LEAR, KENT, NORCLETE, OSWALD, SOLDIERS

LEAR (*in sadness and desperation*): Hold, hold. I am the one you're looking for.
> My misery attests that I am Lear.
> The wronged father stands before you here.

This generous old man, whose zeal you see
Is Kent, whose only crime was loving me.
My daughter spare and he. Let me expire.
Surely that's all my children will require.
Kill me, burn up my whitened locks, I plead
You will be well rewarded for this deed.
(*to* HELMONDE)
Alas our time together was but brief.

HELMONDE:     Could we but die together in our grief.
(*indicating the* SOLDIERS) Go with them, father.

OSWALD:     Come, Cornwall awaits
His enemies delivered to their fates.

## ACT V

*The setting is the same as that of* ACTS III *and* IV.

### Scene 1

#### CORNWALL, OSWALD, GUARDS

CORNWALL (*gives a sign for the* GUARDS *to depart*):
My trusted minister, I have revealed
To you those terrors in my heart concealed
Who my most subtle sign of anger sees
And promptly has removed my enemies.
Dear Oswald, thanks to you this very hour
Lear and his daughter are within my power.
Here in this cavern, far from searching eyes
They laid their plots and spread their treasonous lies.
Hidden in this deep forest, they have sown ...

OSWALD:      Alas, my Lord, we hold Helmonde alone.
She is nearby, but Lear, secure we thought
Has slyly slipped away and not been caught.
But doubtless if we keep his daughter fast
Defeated, he'll return to us at last.
Your soldiers are prepared now for your call.
Edgar it seems has fled, fearing his fall.
Your wife, my Lord, will soon rejoin you here
To share your triumph o'er defeated Lear.

CORNWALL:    Your readiness, dear Oswald, you have shown
To carry out her orders and my own.
Now fate has given me a dictate clear
To dare ... But leave us. Reagan's drawing near.

### Scene 2

#### CORNWALL, REGAN

CORNWALL:    Madam, just now, obeying my commands
Oswald placed Lear and Helmonde in my hands.
We nearly lost. A few scant moments later
Lear might have joined the army of the traitor.

And in that camp his presence would ignite
New ardor and prolong their will to fight.
His hopes took flight when in my arms he fell
And his supporters now are doomed as well.
I have no more to fear.

REGAN:                                    And yet there still
Are many gathered who obey his will.

CORNWALL:    You soon will see them giving up the fight
Rather than share their traitorous leader's plight.
My army's ready. Rebels we need not fear.

REGAN:    But isn't there some danger still from Lear?

CORNWALL:    From an old man, who is half-dead already?
His powers almost gone, his wits unsteady,
Wandering, helpless, only dimly seeing,
Who'd rally to so miserable a being?
He's not the one who stimulates my fears.

REGAN:    It's Helmonde, then?

CORNWALL:                         Indeed. Her sighs, her tears
Will give support to those who are untrue.
She has the same proud lineage as you.
Her suffering, her beauty may inspire
Forces unknown to gather and conspire
Against us, and the steadfast love she's shown
Her father, which by everyone is known
All these give her a fearful power yet.

REGAN:    But surely, Lord, you can beat back her threat?

CORNWALL:    Doubtless I can.

REGAN:                         You must. You surely see
We have no greater enemy than she.
Can you have any doubt she seeks your place
And stirs up adversaries we must face?
Her cruel ambition will engulf this land
With carnage and with blood on every hand.
But worse than conflict is the sly support

> She has within your army and your court.
> Danger is everywhere. See with what art
> She drew Edgar and Lenox from your heart.
> Only these two so far have been revealed
> But traitors' hearts are easily concealed
> And near to you these traitors may disguise
> Their rebel thoughts behind their guileless eyes.
> A change in fortune may come any hour
> And turn against your person your own power.
> Helmonde is still alive. Before presiding
> Over her fate, find out what she is hiding
> Then sadly give the sentence that you must,
> Insisting that her trial has been just
> And thus destroy her who alone can hurt you,
> This phantom symbol with her phantom virtue.
> This is the only remedy. It's clear.

CORNWALL (*as the* GUARDS *appear*):
　　　　Guards, get Helmonde at once and bring her here!

*The* GUARDS *leave.*

REGAN:　　　This all must be resolved without delay
　　　　You understand. Oswald …

CORNWALL:　　　　　　　　　　　　　He will obey
　　　　Whatever I demand.

REGAN (*aside, seeing* HELMONDE *coming*):
　　　　　　　　　　　She comes. I'll hide
　　　　Beneath a smile the wrath I feel inside.


Scene 3

CORNWALL, REGAN, HELMONDE, GUARDS

CORNWALL:　　You're agitated, Madam, and with reason.
　　　　We're well aware of your attempts at treason.
　　　　If you are guilty, you have much to fear.

HELMONDE:    I tremble. You have all the power here.
I've done my duty. I can face my fate.
Only one worry makes me hesitate.
One care disturbs my heart and drives my fears
And 'tis not for myself I shed these tears.
Alas, do what you will with me, but please
Spare the old man before you on his knees
His hoary head inclined, ravaged by grief
Without a witness, let him find relief
A last time in my arms bring him to lie
And in his grave already, let him die.
Pity for me I do not dare to seek
But if the blood within my veins could speak
It would say, sister, only one boon I plead
To succor father in his final need.
He will die soon, then take my life as well.
Not fearing ...

REGAN:                           Wait. You first have much to tell.

HELMONDE:    What do you wish to know?

REGAN:                            What charms were those
That turned my loyal subjects into foes?

HELMONDE:    Alas!

CORNWALL:        Speak, Madam.

REGAN:                        Say what generous heart
Has dared to take the outcast father's part?
Tell all you know of this, or you are lost.

HELMONDE:    I'll not deny my cause, whatever the cost.

REGAN:    There still are secrets that you must reveal.
Your crimes are such ...

HELMONDE:                   I've nothing to conceal.
I love my father, hearing of his pain
I sought revenge, and would do so again.
The court, the people, Edgar all concur.
Heaven and nature my co-rebels were.

CORNWALL:   Who guided you to this deserted lair?
            Speak now.

HELMONDE:                       The gods and lightning brought me there.

CORNWALL:   What convinced Edgar?

HELMONDE:                         My unhappy state.

CORNWALL:   Your cohorts?

HELMONDE:                    Those whom fathers venerate.

CORNWALL:   Their names?

HELMONDE:            I'm silent.

CORNWALL:                         They must be revealed.

REGAN:      The most cruel pains ...

HELMONDE:                        Kill me. My lips are sealed.
            A fate like that I will embrace with pride.
            Crime works in secret, I have naught to hide.
            I have no need your subjects to enflame;
            Their ideals and my own are quite the same.
            They will avenge their fathers and your crime,
            Guided by nature and its will sublime.
            Villains, beware, a crowd against you strives—
            Father and children, husbands and their wives.
            (to CORNWALL)
            Tyrant, you'll answer for my father's fate,
            England your crimes will never tolerate.
            Tremble before the coming judgment day!
            What am I saying? Pardon me I pray.
            Upon my knees I call on you to hear,
            From me and friends of mine you've naught to fear.
            Be clement, Duke, remember in your hate
            That Lear gave you his daughter and his state.
            Ah, sister, put revengeful thoughts aside.
            Recall when you were happy as a bride.
            Respect the gods, do not their laws despise;
            Extend your arms, as I do, toward the skies.

I will forget all pains I have endured,
But love my father and our rift is cured.


## Scene 4

CORNWALL, REGAN, HELMONDE, LEAR, KENT, GUARDS

LEAR (*from offstage*): My daughter, hear me!

HELMONDE (*to* CORNWALL):             Pity him. You see
         Dying, he comes to share his grief with me.
         Alas, you need commit no parricide.

LEAR (*entering in a quiet distraction, full of tenderness*):
         Dear children, heaven has led me to your side.
         (*He places* REGAN *in* CORNWALL'*s arms*.)
         Dear Duke, my own dear blood I give to you
         Without regret, and take *my* scepter too.

HELMONDE:     Here is the foe you'd murder if you could.
         I see his sorrow has touched you, as it should.


## Scene 5

CORNWALL, REGAN, HELMONDE, GUARDS, LEAR, KENT, ALBANY
*and his* GUARDS

ALBANY:       Edgar approaches, leading on our foes
         As he advances, still his army grows.
         Combat is certain; the result I fear.
         They idolize Helmonde and pity Lear.
         Their minds are full of hatred and of wrath
         There is time to seek another path
         And turn aside their growing force before
         These rocks around us are awash in gore.
         My Lord, avoid this bloodshed, spare these lands
         Release Helmonde and Lear into my hands.
         With your support, along with their release
         I'll undertake to organize a peace.
         Edgar will hear me.

CORNWALL:                          And you would betray
                    The honor of the sovereign in this way?
                    Consider my station and my just wrath fear!

ALBANY (*indicating* HELMONDE *and* LEAR)
                    Duke, see your sister and your father here.

CORNWALL:       The name of king means nothing then to you?

ALBANY:         But blood and nature must be honored too.
                    (*indicating* LEAR *and* HELMONDE)
                    So may I take them? Answer. I await.

CORNWALL:       'Tis I alone who must decide their fate.
                    I'll keep them, Sir.

ALBANY:                            And will they be secure?

CORNWALL:       My own tranquility I must insure.

ALBANY:         I have no more to do here. I'll retire.
                    Each has his projects. Do what you desire.
                    May Heaven soon decide between our cases,
                    But we'll no longer see each other's faces.
                    Farewell, my Lord.

CORNWALL:                            Farewell.

ALBANY *leaves with his* GUARDS.


## Scene 6

CORNWALL, REGAN, HELMONDE, LEAR, KENT, GUARDS

CORNWALL:                            I do not fear
                    His threats. The power is mine.


## Scene 7

CORNWALL, REGAN, HELMONDE, LEAR, KENT, STRUMOR, GUARDS

STRUMOR (*to* CORNWALL): Lord, Edgar's near!
Your scattered forces fall before his might
And soon his standards will appear in sight.
All fly before his overwhelming force ...

CORNWALL:     Let's meet this rebel and reverse his course.
You, Regan, listen. (*He speaks low to* REGAN.)

REGAN:                          Understood.

CORNWALL (*to his* GUARDS):                          And you,
(*indicating* LEAR *and* HELMONDE)
Remain, and keep close watch over these two.

*He leaves with* STRUMOR *on one side*, REGAN *on the other.*)

## Scene 8

### HELMONDE, LEAR, KENT, GUARDS

LEAR (*to* HELMONDE *and* KENT): You love me still?

KENT:                          Alas!

HELMONDE:                          Father, I vow
You've never been more dear to me than now.
Whatever is my fate, if I can be
Near you, I'll bear it.

## Scene 9

### HELMONDE, LEAR, KENT, OSWALD, GUARDS

OSWALD (*to* HELMONDE):          Madam, follow me.

HELMONDE (*indicating* LEAR): You wish us both?

OSWALD:                          No, Madam, you alone.

HELMONDE:     Not with him! Terror strikes me to the bone.
Hear me, dear Kent ...

KENT (*trying to hold back his tears*): Alas!

HELMONDE (*her voice low, so that* LEAR *cannot hear her.*):
                                        My faithful friend,
                    Without me, close his dear eyes at the end.
                    Give him your tender care; don't let him know
                    What fate I suffer. Farewell. I must go.

LEAR:               You leave me?

HELMONDE:                           I will soon return to you.

LEAR:               You won't be long?

HELMONDE:                               Adieu, father, adieu.


                            Scene 10

                        LEAR, KENT, GUARDS

LEAR:               Kent, will we meet again?

KENT:                               My Lord I trust
                    Heaven will at the end unite the just.

LEAR:               What happiness! If you and I and she
                    Could be together for eternity!
                    Here crime and pain surround us without cease.
                    The wilderness also provides us peace.
                    (*He believes he sees* HELMONDE *returning.*)
                    Here's the provider dear of all my needs.
                    Come, daughter, sit beside me on these reeds.
                    Were I to lose you, then my life has fled.

## Scene 11

LEAR, KENT, CORNWALL, EDGAR (*in chains*), GUARDS, SOLDIERS

CORNWALL (*holding aloft a bloody sword*):
>
> With my foe's blood my hand and sword are red.
> Mine was the glory, mine the victor's path.
> (*to* EDGAR) Traitor, be sure you won't escape my wrath.
> Lenox is taken too.

EDGAR:
>                                     Abhorrent foe,
> You are the victor, strike the fatal blow.
> Do not delay. I know my doom is near.

CORNWALL:
>
> Your wishes will be granted, never fear.
> I feel no pity, nor sweet nature's power.
> (*to* LEAR) Old man, I'll shut you in an obscure tower.
> (*to* KENT) And you, in irons, will die in that same cell.

LEAR:
>
> But let me daughter be with me as well.

CORNWELL:
>
> She's dead.

LEAR:
>                          My daughter!

EDGAR:
>                                          Horror!

KENT:
>                                               Barbarous act!

EDGAR:
>
> How can your mouth proclaim so foul a fact?

CORNWALL:
>
> Yes, Oswald in her blood has dipped his arms.
> I'll no more fear her plotting or her charms.

LEAR:
>
> Monster, your deed my reason has restored.
> O heavens, I've lost the one I most adored.
> (*He falls, overcome, upon the rocks.*)
> My Helmonde is no more!

CORNWALL (*to his* SOLDIERS):
>                          Take him away.

KENT:
>
> Monster, complete your murderous deeds today!

Rouse yourself, Lear, lean on me as your guide.
Gods, here's the father (*indicating* LEAR).
Here the homicide (*indicating* CORNWALL).
The crown, the day is given to these souls
Who murder children to achieve their goals.

EDGAR (*in* KENT's *arms*): My father!

KENT:                                   Edgar dear!

CORNWALL:                                           Take them away
And separate them.

EDGAR:                                   Villain, I will stay.
How dare you claim yours is the winning side
When even the gods pale at your parricide?
Of all your crimes none of your soldiers brags
But weeps in shame behind dishonored flags.
Helmonde is dead, but her death will inspire
Legions to seek for vengeance in their ire.
Tyrant, your power seems supreme today
But Nature and the gods will have their say.
Indomitable Nature, which, no doubt,
For your inhuman deeds will cast you out.
Soldiers, stand by me!

ONE OF CORNWALL's SOLDIERS (*moving to stand by* EDGAR):
                                   I will heed you call
And fight for you.

*Many of* CORNWALL's SOLDIERS *move to* EDGAR's *side, but a much larger number remain by* CORNWALL, *swords in hand, ready to fight.*

CORNWALL (*to* EDGAR's *party*):     Back, traitors!

EDGAR:                                   Tyrant, fall!
(*to* CORNWALL's SOLDIERS)
Friends, for what monster do you draw your sword?
Covered with Helmonde's blood, by Heaven abhorred
The anger of the gods you all must fear!
(*to* CORNWALL, *indicating* LEAR.)
One crime remains, murder your father, Lear.

LEAR (*coming to himself at the sound of "father," with joy, but still distracted*):
I am.

CORNWALL (*furious*):     Well then!

A SOLDIER:                              Die, fiend!
*He disarms* CORNWALL *and turns his sword back on himself, ready to stab him.*

EDGAR (*seeing the danger to* CORNWALL, *stops the soldier who is about to kill him*):     He is your king!

*All the soldiers desert* CORNWALL *and at once join* EDGAR's *party, falling with respect at* LEAR's *feet. They lower their arms before him and incline their flags.*

CORNWALL:               Where am I?

EDGAR (*to the soldiers at* LEAR's *feet*):               You have done a glorious
thing!
(*to* CORNWALL): You are alone, disarmed, prey to their fury
And I, in irons, am made your judge and jury.
Heaven has spoken. Have you recognized
The power of virtue that you so despised?
Go join the others who have so defiled
Our land. (*to* SOLDIERS) Remove him.


Scene 12

LEAR, KENT, EDGAR, ALBANY, HELMONDE, GUARDS, SOLDIERS

ALBANY (*placing* HELMONDE *in* LEAR's *arms*): Lear, behold your child.
I saw the monstrous Oswald raise his arm
I ran to stop him from committing harm.
In his own blood I drowned him, but I sought
The evil Volnerille and found her not.
She who behind the scenes, where many missed her
Aided the evil schemes of her cruel sister.
The people seized them both and seemed prepared
To tear them limb from limb had they but dared.
Instead they dragged them, shrieking with despair,
To loathsome pits, imprisoning them there.
Their hands impious weighted down with chains,

No sunlight ever cast upon their pains.
Their crimes a cruel death would justify
But thanks to your name, Lord, they did not die.
Your virtues called for clemency and they
Dissolved in tears, put thoughts of death away.
Live, reign, my father.

LEAR:                                   Oh ye gods on high,
(*regarding* HELMONDE) With what a vision you
delight my eye.

HELMONDE:     They have blessed Edgar, giving him the might
To save the innocent, the evil smite.

EDGAR:     Generous sovereign and father tender,
In serving you I have been their defender.

LEAR:     Their justice is profound, beyond reproach.
Approach dear Edgar, dear Helmonde approach.
Receive, my children, with the name of spouse
The title too of sovereign on your house.
Your virtues far surpass an earthly throne.
I give you to each other as your own.
(*to* ALBANY, *pointing out* HELMONDE)
Duke, all to you I owe, your noble deeds
Have brought all happiness, served all our needs.
Oh my dear son, oh hero I adore
Wed my dear daughter; I could wish no more.
(*showing* EDGAR *and* HELMONDE *to* KENT)
Behold our children, guard them well, dear Kent.
And gods, who such stout friends to me have sent,
Before I drift into eternal sleep
Let me a while these blessed friendships keep.
Maintain my reason, oh ye gods above,
But should that fail, preserve my heart to love.

*The curtain falls.*

# OTHELLO

## 1792

# CAST OF CHARACTERS

MONCENIGO

PEZARE

ODALBERT

OTHELLO

HEDELMONE

HERMANCE

LOREDAN

SENATORS

OFFICERS

MEN CARRYING TORCHES

## ACT I

*The stage represents the Senate chamber. The senators are seated on their chairs. Several officers are standing at a distance.*

### Scene 1

### MONCENIGO, SENATORS, OFFICERS

MONCENIGO:    Illustrious senators, cease your alarms.
Warned of its peril, Venice took up its arms,
But those revolts, those torrents of attacks
The bold Othello stopped them in their tracks.
A fire, long-suppressed, fierce flames produced;
Verona was to ashes grim reduced.
But here, deprived of air to give it life,
We suffered but a momentary strife.
Heaven looked on our troubles from afar
And victory ...

### Scene 2

### MONCENIGO, SENATORS, OFFICERS, PEZARE

MONCENIGO:                 Is that you, dear Pezare?
Othello's worthy friend, you must relate
His latest contributions to our state.
Once more his valor has been our salvation.

PEZARE:    Would you had seen how well he served his nation!
The rebels came and he, to push them back,
Ran out alone to parry their attack.
Faster than light he came and took his stand,
Crying "Come friends, defend our fatherland."
Soldiers and citizens, united all
Fought as one man in answer to his call.
In fierce display we saw his visage dark
Upon which Afric's sun had left its mark
And followed his relentless steps with pride
Happy to combat at this hero's side.
The rebel leader, sensing his defeat
Prudently paused and started to retreat.
He made a stand and by a lucky chance
Briefly held back our hasty first advance.
But once again his forces took to flight
And all at last surrendered to our might.

I must return. Should there be some defection
I still have blood to shed for our protection.


## Scene 3

### MONCENIGO, SENATORS, OFFICERS

MONCENIGO:    You see, my Lords, what dangers us surround;
But in great perils great men must be found.
When dangerous times breed heroes of this sort,
We senators must give them our support.


## Scene 4

### MONCENIGO, SENATORS, OFFICERS, ODALBERT

ODALBERT *enters furious and out of control.*

MONCENIGO:    Be calm, dear Odalbert, the danger's past.
Our threatened state is now secure at last.

ODALBERT:     Alas, the suffering you see has grown
Not from the state. My troubles are my own.
My daughter ...

MONCENIGO:                 Well?

ODALBERT:                              My daughter. Ah, what woe!

MONCENIGO:    Is she then dead? Is that what moves you so?

ODALBERT:     'Tis not her death that brings me now to stand
Before this body, justice to demand.
A traitorous seducer has my daughter led
Into corruption and has with her fled.
In secret marriage they have been united,
My wishes scorned, and all convention slighted.

MONCENIGO:    I share your woe. This senate, always fair,
Will find the author of this foul affair.
The bloody sword of law will soon be used
On him who has your family so abused.
What is his name?

## Scene 5

### MONCENIGO, SENATORS, OFFICERS, ODALBERT, OTHELLO

ODALBERT (*pointing to* OTHELLO, *who enters hastily*): That is the
        monster there.

MONCENIGO:                Othello! Gods!

ODALBERT (*to* OTHELLO):            For my revenge prepare!
        (*to* MONCENIGO) Before, however, anyone proceeds
        To strike this ingrate for his evil deeds,
        Before this barbarous African is brought
        To suffer for his trespass as he ought,
        My noble friend, my daughter is nearby
        Let her be called to us to testify.

MONCENIGO (*to two* OFFICERS): Heed Odalbert, answer his supplication
        Bring Hedelmone here, without hesitation.

*The* OFFICERS *leave.*

ODALBERT:      You are a father, Doge, your son has virtue
        And never would commit an act to hurt you.
        He lives abroad, has never had instruction
        In deeds of foul betrayal and seduction.
        In your heir's name, my Doge, I make my plea.
        Respect my age, defend humanity,
        Defend those rights Nature herself bestows
        And this foul monster punish and expose.
        (*to* OTHELLO): Speak now, corruptor, by what evil art
        Have you imposed upon my daughter's heart?
        How have you conquered this sweet innocence,
        So young, so frail, so lacking in defense?
        She whom a thousand suitors woo'd in vain,
        Could such a monster her affections gain?

OTHELLO:      Odalbert, I've been silent all this time.
        It is your right to charge me with this crime.
        But when I was your friend you had no scorn
        To heap upon the place where I was born.
        Now in my face, I beg you, see remorse
        And not the workings of some evil force.
        At birth, alas, the gods in Heaven above
        Gave me a heart too sensible to love.
        That is my crime. Had I the choice, instead
        Of Africa, I would have here been bred.

True, in the desert I first saw the day
But it was not my destiny to stay.
Is African a title so outrageous?
Can one of such a name not be courageous?
I'm called the Moor. I wear that name with pride
And hope its fame endures when I have died.
But now such glory must to love give way,
I'll try to satisfy you if I may;
My blood I'd shed if need be to placate you.
Must my appearance always irritate you?
I have no family, but count my scars.
Think of my sacrifices made to Mars.
Think of my services, which have been great
Think how you've cried, "The Moor has saved our state!"

ODALBERT:       Intrepid actions can barbarians show,
But also perfidy, as I well know.
Your dark designs were hidden from the start
As you prepared the steel to pierce my heart.
Consider, Lords, how families may be wrecked,
If you, like I have daughters to protect.
The same dishonor you may one day face
Protect yourselves revenging my disgrace.
My daughter ... oh, despair! ... whom I adored
You have seduced her. This is my reward.

MONCENIGO:      Othello, speak. It passes my belief
That you would bring a father to such grief.
By what means did you win his daughter to you?

OTHELLO:        A full accounting, Lord, I know is due you.
Within his tranquil palace Odalbert
Urged me the story of my life to share
So I, thinking his envy to assuage
Told him my exploits from my earliest age.
My trials, my battles, hardships that I bore,
My vessel foundering on a foreign shore,
And often on the very brink of death.
And as I spoke, with awe and bated breath
Hedelmone hung on every word I'd say
And when some household task drew her away
Reluctantly to care for it she'd run,
And soon return, her duties quickly done.
And then, with tears and sighs she'd sit enthralled
As I the torments of my life recalled.
One fatal day (permit me to disclose)
Her simple pity, stirred up by my woes,

As I recounted stories of my pains
"Othello," she cried, "you have been bound in chains!
Alas, what fearful pictures you evoke—
Upon your shoulders slavery's heavy yoke!
If only some brave girl could undertake
To bear your woes, or perish for your sake.
Oh if some warrior wanted me to woo,
He'd tell the sort of stories that you do.
My heart would cede to him a victory."
Her innocence and her simplicity
Charmed me, as did the sadness in her eyes
Whose tears she scarcely bothered to disguise.
I saw them. To my own tears she appealed.
The secrets of our hearts were thus revealed.
Her pity for my woes to love was turned
And seeing this, love also in me burned.
These are the means, and these the dangerous arts
That have seduced us both and joined our hearts.


## Scene 6

### MONCENIGO, SENATOR, OFFICER, ODALBERT, OTHELLO, HEDELMONE, HERMANCE

HEDELMONE *is ordered seized by two* OFFICERS.

HEDELMONE: Arrested! What is this?

ODALBERT (*to his daughter, indicating* HERMANCE): Now, go with her.
Aren't you ashamed of making such a stir?
A virtuous girl would shun all this display.

HEDELMONE:    My eyes are dim. My body's giving way.

ODALBERT (*to* HERMANCE): And you who, in my palace, were expected
To see my daughter's innocence protected.
I thank you for your care. I see that she
Had little to constrain her liberty.

HEDELMONE:    Support me, dear Hermance.

ODALBERT (*aside*):                                    My rage hold back.
(*aloud*) Is this your spouse?

HEDELMONE (*aside*):                    How to respond? (*aloud*) Alack!
This warrior, silent now before your blame
Needs not my marriage to increase his fame.
His triumphs are the glories of the nation
His fame resounds through every conversation.
His perils drew me to him from the start.
I don't deny it. Thus he gained my heart.
The tales of one my countrymen adore
I heard with rapture, and I would hear more.
His valor to our ancestors compares.
Should not his race be equal then to theirs?
Revered by you, adored by common men
He has saved Venice, may do so again.
Let your hearts speak, and calm your irritation
I beg you ...

*She throws herself at her father's feet.*

ODALBERT (*stopping her*):        I forbid this supplication.

MONCENIGO:        She begs a father's mercy. Do not spurn
Her tears.

ODALBERT:                            Vengeance is my concern.

MONCENIGO:        What do you want?

ODALBERT:                                    Arrest him.

MONCENIGO:                                            What, our savior?

ODALBERT:        I only see his criminal behavior.

MONCENIGO:        Then let the Senate judge. Think of his fame!

ODALBERT:        A criminal can such attention claim?

MONCENIGO:        Odalbert, try to modify your tone.
The Senate listens. We are not alone.
Would you have us condemn him on the spot?

ODALBERT:        No, justice rarely functions as it ought.

MONCENIGO:        What do I hear?

ODALBERT:                            Unite in his protection
I see this criminal has your affection.

'Tis always thus, statesmen protect their friends
And laws are scorned, to serve their private ends.
(*aside*) But soon ... my vengeance ...

MONCENIGO:                                    Odalbert, hold back!
It is the state itself that you attack.
Your pride and threats expose you as a menace
To everyone, and most of all to Venice.

ODALBERT (*to his daughter*): There still is time; my anger I must
swallow.
(*pointing to* OTHELLO)
Choose then which of us two you now will follow.

HEDELMONE (*looking toward* OTHELLO): My father ...

ODALBERT (*turning to leave*):                        'Tis enough.
You can't disguise
The blindfold he has placed upon your eyes.
I now will ...

MONCENIGO:                    Odalbert!

ODALBERT:                                    Prince, stand aside.
My case is now for Heaven to decide.
(*to* OTHELLO) You fooled me, false deceiver. May you
learn
The sorrow of deception in your turn.
Ingrate, may Heaven so becloud your eyes
That what you take for truth will all be lies.
May nothing in your life be what it seems
And you base all your hopes upon false dreams.
Between the two may you be cast adrift;
Let never certainty your spirits lift.
May paths you trust conduct you to the pit
And seeking virtue, may you crimes commit.
Until at last you meet your shameful doom
And truth will hold its beacon o'er your tomb!
(*to* HEDELMONE): And barbarous child, to your own
blood untrue,
Revenging Heaven will take care of you.
(*to* OTHELLO) Ungrateful wretch, you'll suffer too, I vow.
(*pointing to the band of diamonds on his daughter's
head*)
Your hands have placed this curse upon her brow.
Watch over her. She has her father vexed

With her deception and you may be next.
Remember this. Farewell.

*He goes.*


## Scene 7

MONCENIGO, SENATORS, OFFICERS, OTHELLO, HEDELMONE, HERMANCE

HEDELMONE:                              Me? A deceiver?

MONCENIGO:    His wrath is speaking, you but its receiver.
Though he is violent, his heart is warm;
Nature will bring him calm after this storm.
Othello, your great glory and repute
Establish rights that no one can dispute.
You must now work to reassure your wife
Who cannot be but troubled by this strife.
Remember too that war is still nearby
And on our rebels keep a watchful eye.

OTHELLO:    Oh noble Doge and Senators august,
Odalbert's wrath, I know full well, is just.
I hope that time and your good will somehow
Will soften the resentment he feels now.
In your wise hands I leave our destiny,
Soldier and man is all I claim to be.
Born under savage skies, far from the court,
My education was but crude and short.
In that world, one relies upon the heart,
If I have pleased you, it was not through art.
I never learned to flatter or seduce,
I knew my happiness I must produce.
But indicate where you would have this son
Of Afric plant your flag, and it is done.
May it be said one day: "When Venice sought
To rule the waves, triumphant was her lot.
Hedelmone lived then, and a Moor she wed
Whom Venice to its greatest triumphs led.
The Moor adored her, and her love inspired
Those exploits for which he was so admired."

MONCENIGO:    'Tis thus a great heart nourishes love' s flame.
Go, brave Othello, always be the same.
If Hedelmone's bright eyes have so inflamed you
I know her heart has as her lover named you.
The gentlest passions have a power great

That pays no heed to rank or to estate.
Love, just like Liberty, demands this right
That everyone is equal in its sight.
Forget those affectations pride has sown
In a republic, honor counts alone.
Your name, your family have but little weight
Compared to your great service to the state.

*All leave but* OTHELLO *and* HEDELMONE.


Scene 8

OTHELLO, HEDELMONE

HEDELMONE:      Think you that time will sooth my father's ire?
                He loves us both.

OTHELLO:                          It is my strong desire
                And fondest hope. But calm the fear
                He caused you by his angry outburst here.
                Soon his excessive tone he'll realize
                And see our love with more forgiving eyes.
                But let's thank Heaven for our wedded bliss,
                I never dreamed of having joy like this.
                Could Odalbert have looked into your soul,
                He'd have removed you far from my control.
                Instead, with joy before the altar I
                Swore I would love you 'til the day I die.
                My happiness was won. But now alarms
                Of threats to Venice call me back to arms.
                The secret bonds of marriage guarantee
                That nothing e'er can sever you from me.
                Do you believe my vows?

HEDELMONE:                                How could I not?
                Within Othello's heart my heart is caught.
                But is it also written on your heart
                That my great love for you will ne'er depart?
                Do not my father's warnings give you pause?

OTHELLO:        What, I? If there were e'er the slightest cause
                The least suspicion that disturbed your peace.
                My blood would freeze, my heart to beat would cease.

HELDEMONE:      Your heart is happy then?

OTHELLLO:                              I've often felt
                     Upon my head tempestuous torrents pelt;
                     Upon the raging seas, my wondering eyes
                     Saw lightning strike the waves, and fill the skies.
                     After these tempests, sweet indeed the calm,
                     But far less sweet than love's all-healing balm,
                     Such happiness, such endless joy is this!
                     Surely no man before me felt such bliss.
                     My ravished soul is now so elevated;
                     My happiness is here all concentrated.
                     The joy I feel my heart can scarcely capture
                     Could I die now, then I would die in rapture.
                     Oh you above, who know my voice, restore
                     To her the father that she had before.
                     Let her be happy, since you've let her charms
                     Be now entrusted to these barbarous arms.
                     To guard this treasure, to deserve her love
                     Give me the virtues praised in Heaven above.
                     Inspire in me the fondest love revealing
                     Those joyful transports that I now am feeling.

## ACT II

*The stage represents* OTHELLO's *palace.*

### Scene 1

### HEDELMONE, HERMANCE

HEDELMONE: So, dear Othello, now your home I know,
But still I tremble and my tears still flow!
Oh how much more this place would give me cheer
If father and my husband both were here!

HERMANCE: It was Othello's thought that to succeed
Your marriage must be secret. You agreed.

HEDELMONE: I did and both of us took every care
To keep the watching world quite unaware.
Hermance, from birth it's you I have to thank
For all my care. It was your milk I drank.
How sweet it was whene'er my spirit failed
When my young soul by troubles was assailed.
To meet a heart receptive to my fears,
To sooth my sorrows and to share my tears
My dear Hermance! ...

HERMANCE:                                  Ah, yes, then ...

HEDELMONE:                                         From my birth
You've been my greatest comfort on this earth.

HERMANCE: When first your eyes were opened to the light,
My arms held you; my face was your first sight.

HEDELMONE: Heaven, which helps the innocent, they say,
My sister and my mother took away.
Now I have lost my father too, I fear.

HERMANCE: Eventually his rage will disappear.
Of Heaven's bounty you must never despair.

HEDELMONE: But of my own sin I am now aware.

HERMANCE: Othello's feats will wipe away all stain
And quiet all lingering doubts that may remain.

HEDELMONE:    It's said that he is gone to seek new dangers
Across the seas, in the domains of strangers.

HERMANCE:    He'll soon return and claim his loving wife.

HEDELMONE:    If he is not shipwrecked, or slain in strife.

HERMANCE:    Come purge your heart of images like those.

HEDELMONE:    I love him and I fear. Do you suppose,
Hermance, that were my long departed mother living
She'd bring my father to be more forgiving?

HERMANCE:    I do.

HEDELMONE:          When at his loss I weep again,
Hermance, you always can assuage my pain.

HERMANCE:    There was a time, far from these walls, when I
In deepest sorrow watched my father die.
I held him at the last, my hand did close
His eyes. Oft have I told you of these woes.
But until now you've given me no clue
Of how your mother's loss affected you.
How could you hide from me so deep a feeling?

HEDELMONE:    This inner woe I could not bear revealing.
Now since my love has caused my father to sever
Our ties, she seems more close to me than ever.
I fear I have deserved my misery.

HERMANCE:    My Hedelmone, don't hide your tears from me.

HEDELMONE:    My dear Hermance, from my first steps you've seen
How calm my childhood was and how serene.
Under my mother's guidance and the gaze
Of sister dear, in love I spent those days.
But all too soon Heaven's clouds began to thicken;
My mother by a fatal ill was stricken.
Each day I saw her vital forces fail,
Her face, still youthful, sunken grew, and pale.
Each moment she grew weaker, it was clear,
I still remember, that the end was near.
A frightful vision then she seemed to see,
She turned her sorrowing countenance toward me.
It seemed her soul, its final hour at hand
Foresaw a future that it could not stand.

She cried in fright, "Oh, offspring of my womb,
Come with me, join me in the peaceful tomb.
Fate has disclosed to me at my last breath
That you will die a most unhappy death!"
At these words, she attempted, it appeared
To shield me from the destiny she feared.
It was as if her troubled soul detected
Over my head some menace unsuspected.
With trembling arms she seized and held me fast
As we embraced, her poor heart beat its last.
"Daughter," she gasped and at the end she cried:
"You'll die unhappy." With these words she died.

HERMANCE:    You tremble!

HEDELMONE:                  Yes, my heart cannot be stilled.
I fear one day those words will be fulfilled.

HERMANCE:    Take heart.

HEDELMONE:                 I've lost the one who gave me birth.
No family, no friend upon this earth.
Hermance, don't leave me.

HERMANCE:                  Leave you? Never fear
Into the tomb I'd go with you, my dear.
Until your last breath I'll be by your side
And all the love and comfort I'll provide
As if I were your mother and had heard
Your first sharp cry at birth and your first word.
I feel such love that were you to commit
A crime so great that Heaven blanched at it,
Your punishment upon myself I'd take.
Your fears of this vain prophecy forsake!
Your lord Othello is this country's pride
Conquering all our foes on every side.
His merits and his deeds have made him great,
Without recourse to family or fate.
Dare to compare his glory if you will,
With nobles who've done nothing, or done ill.
Though born of famous fathers, they've no fame
Save what they borrow from the family name.
Come now. If Heaven should be so severe,
Your father, with his pride, has more to fear.
And not your love Othello, who has clearly
Eyes but for you and surely loves you dearly.
Ah, if a heart of innocence can trust

That Heaven and the universe are just
And will protect the faithful and the true,
Much happiness must be in store for you.

HEDELMONE:    Your happy prophecies remove all strife
You have restored my hope, my joy, my life ...
I hear a noise.

HERMANCE:                I must go see.
It is my duty vigilant to be.
Wait here ...

*She goes.*

Scene 2

HEDELMONE alone.

HEDELMONE:    Ah, dear Hermance, my faithful friend.
How much upon your kindness I depend!
I need it much, for frequently I seem
Exposed to ills of which I never dream.
From birth my grateful heart has ever striven
To thank you for the comfort you have given.

Scene 3

HEDELMONE, HERMANCE

HERMANCE:    Madame, an unknown person begs your ear.
He seems almost consumed by grief or fear.
His voice, his grace, his youth, his misery
All urge me to attend unto his plea.

HEDELMONE:    Then bid him enter.
(HERMANCE *leaves to find the young man.*)
                    Suffering as I do,
I would give aid to other sufferers too.

HERMANCE *brings in the young man and then withdraws.*

## Scene 4

### HEDELMONE, LOREDAN

HEDELMONE: Although this visit, Sir, is unexpected,
Your wish to speak to me should be respected.
If you have troubles that are hard to bear,
Your burdens, if I can, I'll gladly share.
Speak, then, and let me know what brings you here.
I know that fate can deal us blows severe.
If you, so young, are suffering some grief,
What can I do to bring you some relief?

LOREDAN: Relief? No, Madame, in my situation
Fate has removed all chance of reparation.
All hope is lost, and adding to my curse
Even your pity makes my suffering worse.

HEDELMONE: Tell me your story.

LOREDAN:                         At war's first alarms,
Against the enemy I took up arms.
I sought to die in glory, but a truce
Was signed before I could be put to use.
My hopes were thwarted, but the rumors spread
Venice had planned a secret war instead.
Ships were prepared to leave for far-off shores,
Othello at their head, for distant wars.
His army, it was said, he had selected
Among those youth in Venice most respected.
I looked for danger, and it seems to me
That I'm full worthy of this company.
Would you petition him to heed my prayers?

HEDELMONE: Why should you want to mix in such affairs?
Alas! Upon the dangers cast your eye.
Tell me, what are you looking for?

LOREDAN:                                  To die.

HEDELMONE: Nothing can turn you from the path you choose?

LOREDAN: To stop my pain, this life I have to lose.

HEDELMONE: Can you, so young, conceive of no relief ...

LOREDAN: Youth often is the time of greatest grief.

HEDELMONE:       Ah, my own life shows me what you endure.
                 Everyone knows my sorrows, I am sure.

LOREDAN:         They do.

HEDELMONE (*aside*):       Alas, my tragic situation
                 Has entered into public conversation!
                 (*aloud*) Alas, and do I have at least some pity?

LOREDAN:         Your love is understood throughout the city.
                 All sympathize, and all anticipate
                 That if your father's rage does not abate ...

HEDELMONE:       Go on.

LOREDAN:                     He may commit some act that clearly
                 Requires the state to punish him severely.

HEDELMONE:       Heaven!

LOREDAN:                     His rage is under observation.
                 He might be killed as dangerous to the nation.

HEDELMONE:       Killed! Pity me, dear Sir, my heart is breaking,
                 You know our laws, the risk that he is taking.
                 Ah pity these two suffering hearts you find
                 In innocence so deeply intertwined.
                 If Nature's cry has touched your heart as well
                 And love's sweet pleasures caused that heart to swell,
                 Then aid me, in the name of that affection.
                 Save my dear father, give him your protection.
                 This gracious aid, in saving him from strife
                 Will save me also, will preserve my life.
                 Heaven has surely placed you in my way
                 To save my father and myself today.
                 Do not refuse my wishes to fulfill.
                 Run, fly to help him. There remains time still.
                 Regard my tears, my terror is complete.
                 I beg your pity, falling at your feet.

LOREDAN:         You, at my feet! Madam, I beg you rise.
                 Your cause is mine, I swear. Come, dry your eyes.
                 You have my word, on me you can rely.
                 I am resolved to live now, not to die.
                 Beg me no more, you only will I serve;
                 Your father's threatened life I will preserve

As if he were my own. You can rely
On me. I'll find him and remain close by.
If need be, I will die in his defense
And your esteem will be my recompense.


## Scene 5

### HEDELMONE, LOREDAN, OTHELLO, PEZARE

OTHELLO *and* PEZARE *appear at this moment at the rear of the stage, seeing* LOREDAN *from afar. They watch him and* HEDELMONE *attentively, but they are so far away that they cannot see his features clearly.*

LOREDAN (*continuing*): I'll soon return when I have more to tell.

HEDELMONE:     Sir, I'll await.

LOREDAN:                         Farewell, Madame.

HEDELMONE:                                     Farewell.

LOREDAN *and* HEDELMONE *go off in opposite directions.* OTHELLO *follows them with his eyes until they are out of sight, as does* PEZARE.


## Scene 6

### OTHELLO, PEZARE

OTHELLO (*pointing after* LOREDAN): Who is he?

PEZARE:                                     We were rather far away,
            His features were unclear, but I would say
            He was a young man.

OTHELLO (*low and aside*): What could this imply?
            Pezare? What do you say to this?

PEZARE:                               Lord, I
            Have no idea.

OTHELLO:                   Still, weren't you aware
            That some o'erwhelming sorrow they seemed to share?
            I could upon their faces tears discern.

PEZARE:        Call Hedelmone and tell her your concern.

OTHELLO:       Why fear her tears? Her soul is pure, I know.
               All surely must be innocent, I know.
               In her good heart there's nothing to suspect.
               I know I have her love and her respect.
               Question her? No, Pezare, in her I see
               A virtue unexcelled in purity.
               It's not her beauty that I most admire,
               But her true heart, which burns with quiet fire
               And with a quiet courage, deep and tender
               That calls on me to cherish and defend her.
               You know me, friend, and you have seen me take
               Up arms in battle for my country's sake.
               Born free, I youthful to the army came
               Where kindly fate heaped glory on my name.
               'Twas all I sought, ne'er dreaming that one day
               My independent heart would so give way
               To love, and all those lofty aspirations
               Gave way before my heart's solicitations
               And I became as new. It was, I vow,
               As if I'd not existed until now.
               Such transports my poor heart had never known!
               Ah, for a glance, a word from Hedelmone
               I'd give up all those honors, all those laurels,
               The petty triumphs gained in martial quarrels.
               Love, dear Pezare, though you may not believe it
               Has brought me to scorn glory and to leave it
               Behind me. Friend, I see your eye admonishing.
               You find such an excess of love astonishing.
               Perhaps her charm your heart has yet to find.
               The evil you have suffered makes you blind.
               Friend, now, beneath these flags, my heart must yield;
               I must return with sadness to the field.
               If I return triumphant and in peace
               Will Odalbert his war against me cease?
               Surely my triumphs ...

PEZARE:                                  Don't rely on those.
               Trust in your friend, who well these people knows,
               They are united only in their greed;
               The lust for power is their only creed.
               Equality they long ago destroyed
               And liberty the people once enjoyed.
               Whatever laws exist they've rendered mute,
               While making their own power absolute.
               The people to the heavens honor you

But to these lords, you're but a parvenu.

OTHELLO: So insolent a term I find revealing
Of how these nobles think with whom they're dealing.
I'll teach them that a soldier parvenu
Despite their insolence, has power too.
They were intelligent to base their fame
On the foundation of their family name.
That's all they have to boast about, these jesters.
They have no merits, only proud ancestors.
But I, a proud son of the desert waste,
Upon my deeds alone my fame is based.
Devoid of fear I go, without remorse,
Secure in my own liberty and force.
Yet Odalbert I must confess has shown
To me as kind a heart as I have known.
Cruel rigor does not hold him in its thrall.
His heart is open still to Nature's call.

PEZARE: His pride out-weighs his sympathy by far
And Odalbert will never ...

OTHELLO: Dear Pezare,
Time presses, this same day I must appear
Before him and prove my love sincere.
I'll swear to him that we will both hold true
To all those rights that are to fathers due.
I greatly fear the anger that he's shown
Has won him enemies, and it's well known
That the authorities may seem to sleep
But careful vigilance they always keep.
They move in shadows, every footstep planned,
Silent and masked, a dagger in their hand.
Your thoughts as much as crimes may rouse their fear,
And soon enough you'll simply disappear.
In deep dark cells their victims are interred,
Where their laments and cries are never heard.
If an offensive word or glance they see,
Vengeance, not justice, is their remedy.
Thus many a citizen in darkness perishes,
His fate unknown to those whom most he cherishes.
Blood flows, death comes, all in a silence deep,
And those who torture their dark secrets keep.
I tremble at the threat to Odalbert.

PEZARE: Another threat also demands your care.
With lust is Venice always occupied

And that with fury often is allied.
Trust is uncertain here, betrayal sure.
Your claim to Hedelmone is not secure.
Make firm your marriage.

OTHELLO:                                    Dear and faithful friend.
You're right. This cloak of secrecy must end.
Before an altar and in Heaven's sight,
With you as witness, we our troth will plight.
Amid the camps, when first our arms we bore,
The two of us eternal friendship swore.
Within our hearts we called each other brother.
Our contract was sealed there, we need no other.
Whatever blows are dealt to us by fate.
We warrior friends will never separate.

## ACT III

### Scene 1

#### HEDELMONE, HERMANCE

HERMANCE:     Madam, of spying eyes you must beware
Of that young man you spoke to, have a care.
Keep this a secret only we two know.
Othello knows not of it, keep him so.

HEDELMONE:     Why hide it?

HERMANCE:                                 Since his passion's clear to see,
Don't give him any cause for jealousy.
The slightest spark that penetrates his soul
May cause a fatal fire we can't control.
Heed the advice I give you and respect it.
Danger may lurk just where you least expect it.
And often those who keep themselves prepared
Are thus from many tears and sufferings spared.

HEDELMONE:     You're like a mother to me, dear Hermance.
Advise me still and nothing leave to chance.
My father's fate still causes me concern.

HERMANCE:     I'll seek his faithful friends and try to learn
The fate of him for whom you deeply care
And will return when I have news to share.

*She leaves.*

### Scene 2

#### HEDELMONE *alone.*

HEDELMONE:     My courage fails. Alas, I know not why.
A dark cloud seems to cover all the sky.
I ask my heart what causes it such fear
And it responds by tremblings more severe.
It fears a heavy tempest may be brewing
That promises to end in my undoing.
Ah, Father, under your watchful eye I spent
A carefree infancy of deep content.
If you should perish! I can ne'er forgive
A state that does not suffer you to live!

May Heaven help me to alleviate
This threat to him, or else to share his fate.
One comes! It is the suffering young stranger.
At least he has not put his sire in danger.
While I ...


Scene 3

HEDELMONE, LOREDAN

HERMANCE *escorts in* LOREDAN, *then retires.*

HEDELMONE:                Oh, unknown youth, I'm much distressed
Have you learned aught to set my mind at rest?
My father ...

LOREDAN:                News disturbing. It is said
Far from the state and city he has fled.
His words outraged the Senate, but the worst
Is that throughout the state his name is cursed.
And there are rumors widely circulating
That with our foes he is negotiating.

HEDELMONE:  Impossible. My father well I know.
His anger in intemperate words he'll show,
But 'gainst our state I know he'll never side
For which our ancestors have lived and died.
This is his heritage; he will obey it.
You outrage him to think he would betray it.

LOREDAN:  I do believe you, and I understand
Even in rage he loves his fatherland.
But you alone can bring him to his senses
Against your sighs he can have no defenses.
Peace will return and dissipate your fears
And love and marriage wipe away your tears.
But I, despairing, seek no such release,
I hate my life, and long for it to cease.
Ah! Madame, have you asked Othello for
That single boon from him that I implore?
Can I go with him to the battle's fire
And win the glorious death that I desire?

HEDELMONE:  I will fulfill the promise I have made.
He soon will know the courage you've displayed,
Your sadness and your youth. Who could deny

A hero who is not afraid to die?
Still pity for your plight holds me from speaking.
Can it be truly death that you are seeking?
Why must you to so sad a fate aspire?

LOREDAN: Now more than ever that is my desire.

HEDELMONE: Have you upon this earth a father living?

LOREDAN: Yes, Madame.

HEDELMONE: Think what pain to him you're giving.

LOREDAN: I'm driven by despair, all reason lost.

HEDELMONE: Leave not your home. Consider well the cost.

LOREDAN: Within the universe I see no balm.
Alas, there was a time my heart was calm ...

HEDELMONE: My Lord, trust me. I'll help you if I may.
Your name, your rank. Reveal yourself, I pray.

LOREDAN: I cannot, Madam.

HEDELMONE: Why? What do you fear?
Where did your father raise you? Was it here?

LOREDAN: Madame a stranger took me in his care.

HEDELMONE: A stranger? Why?

LOREDAN: In Heaven's name I swear
My father sought my safety, there's no doubt.
Fearing a murderer's hand would seek me out
In these our civil wars, a virtuous friend
Promised to raise me and protection lend.
In his retreat my childhood days were spent
Far from society's warlike intent.
In those bucolic haunts I was surrounded
By happy families and joy unbounded.
In gentle happiness they passed their life
Respecting Nature and devoid of strife.
This peaceful life, however, with its charms
At length began to ring with war's alarms.
I was entranced by bold Othello's story;
I left my home so seek him in his glory.

I came to Venice, saw the celebrations,
The flags, and treasures of defeated nations.
I'd never seen such pomp, such marches glorious.
The Senate cheered their hero all-victorious.
Soldiers and banners, everything in motion,
The people surging like a mighty ocean.
Exploding fireworks darkness put to flight
And made the sky a vast display of light.
Othello, modest hero of the hour
Seemed unaware of his exalted power.
And as I watched, enchanted and enraptured,
My roving eye a fair young woman captured.
All other splendors faded from me, while
The gates of Heaven opened with her smile.
My soul that instant came to understand
My life and fate were hers but to command.
My love, aroused, I could not put away;
Her image stayed to haunt me night and day.
I fled beyond the Apennines but there
It followed me, and in the desert air
I saw it, in the floods and savage skies
I could not purge it from my weeping eyes.
Then came the news that all my hopes were dead.
She loved, was loved, and with her love was wed.
My fate was sealed then, all my hopes expired.
I need but add 'twas you that I desired.

HEDELMONE:    What words are these? What thoughts have you
disclosed?
To such outrages am I now exposed?
Think you my heart, so battered by what's past
Has lost all sense of virtue at that last?
Putting aside the love I bear my mate,
My honor, I presume, is past debate.
I can't believe, my lord, that it is true
That I have heard a vow of love from you.
My much-offended duty must implore
You to depart and never see me more.

LOREDAN:    Madam, I've merited such wrath, it's true.

Scene 4

HEDELMONE, LOREDAN, ODALBERT

LOREDAN *seeing* ODALBERT, *retires to the rear of the stage.*

ODALBERT:         Let's listen.

HEDELMONE:                         Oh, my father, it is you!
Your face is deathly pale, your features stark,
Old age and suffering have left their mark!

ODALBERT:         Why speak of suffering, which you brought about?
Why speak of age, when you have cast me out?
My misery, your crime rest on your brow.
What right have you to call me father now?
And yet I feel that it is not too late.
I've come to save you from your guilty state.
I know my rights. There still is ample time
To save you from this man and from this crime.
He is not yet your husband, he can still
Accede to honor's promptings, if he will.
If any family loyalty still ties you,
I can still as my daughter recognize you.
All's ready. Follow me.

HEDELMONE:                         Is it then known
What troubles out of my poor love have grown?

ODALBERT:         We are both blamed, you as a timid prey
An artless soul a villain led astray.
Alas, at that cruel time when all was known,
My love for you by hate was overthrown.
Seeing you now my wrath evaporates
And now in your sweet face I see the traits
Of your beloved sister and my wife
Now resting in their tombs, devoid of life.
Now what is left as I draw near my end?
Despair and tears, no family, no friend.

HEDELMONE:         Dear father!

ODALBERT:                         Yes, as my tears witness bear
Think of my tender love, my loving care.
With what delight your childhood years I viewed;
With all my hopes my infant was imbued.
Soldier and senator, early and late,

I was devoted to my home and state.
My children and my country then combined,
Domestic love and civic in my mind.
Come to yourself, my child, your wits regain,
Recall the home you loved, and there remain.
Recall again our glorious history,
The twenty Doges in our family tree.
They say to you, "Under our sovereignties
The ships of Venice came to rule the seas.
'Twas us, when Rome was conquered and enslaved
Whom dying Liberty took up and saved."
Recall your sister, so soon brought to death;
Your mother, giving you her dying breath.
Of all my family, only you are left.
Would you of father's name leave me bereft?
I wish for you a marriage full of beauty
Where I can hold your torch, as is my duty.
That's my desire.

HEDELMONE:              Alas!

ODALBERT                      Come now.

HEDELMONE:                            Ah, no!
Othello would expire were I to go.

ODALBERT:    Think of yourself.

HEDELMONE:              I do so. You must see
I bear a hundred times more guilt than he.
Though innocently, I gave him instruction
In how to engineer my own seduction.
I was the one who deepened our relations
And drew him into lengthy conversations.
'Twas I who caught his eye, my own o'erflowing
Turning my charms on him, although unknowing.
Thus by degrees, love took us by assault.
Your friend was virtuous. It was my fault.

ODALBERT:    It angers me the more that you defend him.
When this foul traitor got me to befriend him.
He found the most profound device to hurt me
By leading my own daughter to desert me.
Believing my inevitable rage
By offering of marriage he'd assuage.
He scarcely knew the depth of his offense.

HEDELMONE:     Father ...

ODALBERT:                         No more. My plans are made long since.

HEDELMONE:     Consider ...

ODALBERT:                         You'd defend this rogue perfidious?
His very name I now regard as hideous.
Come, sign this letter.

HEDELMONE:                         What is your design?

ODALBERT:     You see this dagger? I will use it! Sign!

HEDELMONE (*aside*): What must I do? O God!

*She signs blindly and hastily, then returns the paper to her father.*

ODALBERT:                         I am delighted.
Our sundered family you have reunited.
My friends support you. Heaven will provide
A hero fit for standing at your side,
A fine young man, devoid of any taint,
Honest, a model, Nature's very saint.
Whose grandeur Venice has yet to behold
But for whom a great future is foretold.
His father has assured me of his worth.
'Tis Loredan, a youth of highest birth
The Doge's son.

HEDELMONE (*aside*):          Oh Heaven! (*aloud*) Can it be
My lord, that he has set his heart on me?

LOREDAN (*coming forward from the rear of the stage where he has
          hidden*): Yes, Madame, my devotion I declare
By Heaven and your beauteous self I swear.
My fire, my faith, my love all testify
That Loredan, the Doge's son, am I.

ODALBERT:     'Tis he indeed.

HEDELMONE (*to* LOREDAN):          My Lord!

ODALBERT:                         Both love and pride
In his high birth should draw you to his side.
Come, daughter, since you now are in my care,
I give you to him.

LOREDAN (*with joy*):                    Rapture!

HEDELOMONE (*to* LOREDAN):                    Can you dare! ...

ODALBERT            Ignore her tears, her anger, her confusion.
                   (*He puts* LOREDAN's *hand into the hands of his
                   daughter.*)
                   Join hands. Young man, thank me for this conclusion,
                   And be my son.

LOREDAN:                               My Lord! Her face grows pale.
                   Her limbs are trembling, her spirits fail!

ODALBERT (*to* LORDAN): Why in your hand is her hand so unsteady?

HEDELMONE:         Do you not know my heart is given already?

ODALBERT:          Without my leave, there can be no proposal.
                   Your heart and hand are both at my disposal.

HEDELMONE:         And what, my Lord, remains of Nature's part?

ODALBERT:          It speaks most clearly in a father's heart.
                   It bids you to remember, as you should,
                   That all we do, we do for your own good.

HEDELMONE:         What must I do?

ODALBERT:                          Obey.

HEDELMONE:                              Is my fate sealed?
                   Othello ... never ...

ODALBERT:                               Choose.

HEDELMONE:                                  My father ...

ODALBERT:                                               Yield!

HEDELMONE:         My blood is yours, it would be shed for you
                   And yet Othello is my husband too.

ODALBERT:          Then I am free. All family I lack
                   I tried in vain to win my daughter back.
                   I blush to think on my erroneous path
                   (*He gives back to* HEDELMONE *the letter he forced her to
                   sign. She takes it.*)

Take back your letter. I take back my wrath.
Go cherish that ingrate whom I abhor.
The deep abyss beneath your feet ignore.
But it will open. Go. Fear not my hate.
Follow the path of your unworthy mate.
I give you to him, to his cruel care.
Family, duty, state, I here forswear.
I've nothing more to lose. Adieu. Discover
The tiger you have taken for your lover.

*He goes.*


## Scene 5

### HEDELMONE, LOREDAN, HERMANCE

HEDELMONE:    He flees me!

*Trembling, she reads the letter her father has given her.*

LOREDAN:                    Courage! Heaven, I am sure
Won't let so sad a parting long endure.

HEDELMONE:    What have I read ... my father ...


## Scene 6

### HEDELMONE, LOREDAN, HERMANCE

HERMANCE:                                Every hour
Your father's enemies increase in power.
Before he saw you, his unlawful acts
Roused protest and exposed him to attacks.
He may escape, but still his peril is great.
Its full details I'm fearful to relate!
Flight, shame, and poverty are all that's left.
A Senate ruling has left him bereft
Of goods and honors, even of the name
Of citizen, and added to this shame.
The fearful Group of Ten has met an said
Nothing will satisfy them but his head.
You can not save him now. No person can.

HEDELMONE:    Heaven, my Lord, inspires me with a plan.
Your father loves you. He alone has power

To save my father in his darkest hour.
As Doge, his power is excelled by none;
As father he must wish to please his son.
Ah, if these marriage plans were under way
That surely would occasion some delay.
My Lord, this letter, signed by me, reveals
My choice and our impending nuptials seals!
My tears and your own prayers will bring about
My father's pardon, I can have no doubt.
My heart condemns this lie, but I must choose
To still its protests or my father lose.
Your vows, your virtue have not this deserved
And yet my father's life must be preserved.
Take now this letter. Use it as you must.
(*She gives him the letter*.)
My life, my fate I thus place in your trust.
I do this gladly, for I feel in you
A noble heart and disposition true.
It's clear to me that you delight indeed
In helping fellow creatures in great need.
My father, Sir, (I cannot bear the thought)
In poverty's vile clutches has been caught.
To aid him in this terrible distress
I'd give the little goods that I possess.
(*Removing a diamond headband that she wears*.)
Take now this band and to it I would add
All of the wealth the Indies ever had,
To boost its value, but must raise instead
Its value by the tears I on it shed.
Before I leave you, sir, let me impart
This last fond offering from my suffering heart.
Fly now. I know for generous souls, my Lord,
That helping others is its own reward.

LOREDAN:    I gladly will accept this undertaking.
It matters not that my own heart is breaking.
This is the pledge that I will make to you,
This marriage odious I will pursue.
The barbarous spectacle will be my aim
Despite my feelings, trembling in shame,
Despite the heavy burdens that I carry,
I'll follow any path that's necessary
To bring you to the altar as you choose.
And thus the loved one I adore, I lose.
I rush to serve you, 'tis the choice I've made
And yet the price is fearful that I've paid.
Don't thank me, Madam; that would not be fitting.

I love you, I am jealous, I'm committing
A crime. What am I saying? 'Tis not true
That I would lay the blame for this on you
But on another. My despair turns back
Upon myself. All confidence I lack.
I promise nothing. Cherish no illusion
About a heart where all is in confusion.

*He goes.*

## Scene 7

### HEDELMONE, HERMANCE

HEDELMONE:   Ah Heaven, what threats! My dear Hermance, it seems
At every step cruel fate destroys my dreams;
His jealous transports raise in me great fear!
With what grim looks he parted from us here.
But do you think that he could take delight
In witnessing my tears, my trembling fright?
His passion is extreme, I can't dispute it
But could he face a crime, or execute it?
I can't believe it. He was born magnanimous.
But he is young, and has a lover's animus.
He might ... Only Othello, in this time of strife
Can rescue both his marriage and his wife.

## Scene 8

### HEDELMONE, HERMANCE, OTHELLO

OTHELLO:   The altar's ready. Come.

HEDELMONE:                                    My father will
Protest.

OTHELLO:             He sets you free.

HEDELMONE:                                    I'm troubled still
By all this mystery. My fears awaken.

OTHELLO:   Pezare assures me.

HEDELMONE:                                    What if he's mistaken?

OTHELLO:        I know your caution, but there is no need.

HEDELMONE:     Delay one day.

OTHELLO:                              Come, follow where I lead.

HEDELMONE:     Hermance!
                (*to* Othello): One day!

OTHELLO:                              Give in to my demands!

HEDELMONE:     One day!

HERMANCE: (*in a low voice, to* HEDELMONE): Give in.

HEDELMONE (*following* OTHELLO *out*):            Gods, I am in your
                hands.

*All leave.*

# ACT IV

## Scene 1

### OTHELLO, PEZARE

**OTHELLO:** What! Once again my marriage plans are thwarted.
My bride is at the very altar courted!
What treason's this? An unknown rival stands
Beside and would tear her from my hands!

**PEZARE:** Let peace descend, and put aside your fear.
Heaven spared Hedelmone and she is here.
Heaven will see your happiness complete.

**OTHELLO:** To wrest her from me at the altar's feet?
What monster has imposed on me this menace?

**PEZARE:** I've said already. We reside in Venice.

**OTHELLO:** Old Odalbert I know would find great pleasure
In wrenching from my arms my greatest treasure.
But he's not here and at this sight distressing
I see but you, who somehow can stand by
And view this outrage with a peaceful eye.
Do you know who this strange young man might be
Who has appeared here so mysteriously?

**PEZARE:** No, in this dark retreat, his features dim,
I tried, but I could not distinguish him.
But when before the altar some disturbance
Distracted for a moment your observance,
His mask perfidious revealed a bit
Of an intrepid youth concealed by it.
A desperate, tortured soul who had decided
To die if he were from his love divided.
Although the traitor's features were not clear
I think I'd know him, were he to appear.

**OTHELLO:** My friend, my mind is calmer now. I see
That Hedelmone deserves her liberty.
She is of noblest birth, and is among
The tenderest of souls, and she is young.
I trust her love, and yet I realize
Another could attract her youthful eyes.
I am a soldier, trained in war and arms

Not a young lover full of grace and charms.
Another may have gained her approbation.

PEZARE:    Her family ranks highly in the nation
Of noble birth, endowed with beauty's gift,
She's at an age when passions quickly shift.
A father to disarm, another mate
At hand ... Her course, who can anticipate?

OTHELLO:    Hedelmone beautiful and young may be,
But still I trust her to be true to me.

PEZARE:    I think so too.

OTHELLO:                    Do you?

PEZARE:                                        This very day
Her actions will reveal she's as you say.

OTHELLO:    So I believe ... and you?

PEZARE:                                        She can't disguise
Her feelings. You may read them in her eyes.
Does she avoid your glance?

OTHELLO:                                        I can't deny it,
Yet she continues watching me in quiet.

PEZARE:    Those new to love and trying to conceal it
Will by that effort frequently reveal it.
Have you no other troubles you can share?

OTHELLO:    No, nothing.

PEZARE:                        Speak, my friend.

OTHELLO (*aside*):                                        I do not dare.

PEZARE:    Well?

OTHELLO:                        As I sought to lead her to the altar,
I saw her eyes cast down, her footsteps falter.
A trembling seized her limbs; I did not know
What troubled her and could distress her so.
And as if she were daring my displeasure,
She had removed a gift she knows I treasure,
Her diamond headband, and she keeps nearby

A strange young man, and does not tell me why.
What can the cause of these strange actions be?

PEZARE: My dearest friend, beware of jealousy!

OTHELLO: Continually my apprehensions grow!
I merely wish at last the truth to know.
Tell me, do you consider this young man
Will satisfy his ardor if he can?
Hide nothing from me. Speak. Think you he will
Succeed?

PEZARE: When love's involved, virtue is still.
Its power is mighty, easy is defeat.
You tremble, Lord?

OTHELLO: No, I am in complete
Control. You think ... ?

PEZARE: That he alone has erred,
Outraged your love by this conduct absurd.

OTHELLO: If Hedelmone, unfaithful, placed that band,
My gift, in this unworthy rival's hand!
The desert lions, in rage beyond belief
Bring passing travelers to bloody grief.
Yet 'twould be better for these beasts to tear
Your flesh than to be forced to bear
The tortures I'd inflict when in my wrath.

PEZARE: You make me tremble!

OTHELLO: If this is his path.
I'll follow him and at the proper time
Select a torment proper to his crime.
And offer him, a bloody sacrifice
Unto the one he plotted to entice.

PEZARE: My Lord, unleash your rage on him alone
I fear now for the life of Hedelmone!

OTHELLO: Fear not. Fear not.

PEZARE: Before you judge, review
All that she's given up for love of you.
She loves. But who? Could there be any danger
That she's been swept away by this young stranger?

How do you think her beauty's put to use?
To stimulate pure love, or to seduce?
She trembles, is that reason for attacking?
Upon her modest brow your band is lacking.
Seek not in proofs like these her vindication,
But in her heart and in her reputation.
That heart is generous and vice prefers
To test its wiles on beauty such as hers.
To view her jealously would be unjust.
When she is virtuous, in her virtue trust.
Meek Hedelmone, with what can you reproach her?
For loving you, her father won't approach her.
Take my advice, Othello, leave these climes;
Go where you've won renown in happier times.
Expand the realm of Venice to the East
From jealousy and local cares released.
Your passion here may cause more devastation
Than raging floods or fearsome conflagration.
Lead Hedelmone to some far Asian shore
Where you can wed and love her evermore.
Perform such deeds that even Odalbert
Must honor you and claim you as his heir.
To his vain pride in lineage and name
Oppose your glories and your growing fame.
This is the proper jealousy for you,
Your followers stand ready, as I do.
But if, against my wishes, I perceive
This would-be ravisher before we leave
Wandering in the streets around the palace,
I guarantee he won't escape my malice.
Once recognizing him, I will not rest
Until my dagger's buried in his breast.
In this revenge I will fulfill my duty
Unto my friend, to virtue, and to beauty.

*He goes.*

## Scene 2

### OTHELLO *alone.*

OTHELLO:    I breathe again! Yes, in Pezare I'm given
The rarest friend by an indulgent Heaven.
His cooler reason furnishes the balm
That serves my too-impetuous heart to calm!
Were he in love, he'd practice such control

That he would be the emperor of his soul.
Were he not kindly, there could surely be
No one more cold and treacherous than he.
Has he not sometimes glanced with love upon
My Hedelmone? Suspicion foul, begone!
Oh wretch, cannot your closest friend admire
Those very charms to which you most aspire?
There is no doubt. He's taken her defense
Because he's certain of her innocence.
I'll follow his advice and take my dear
To some place that is far removed from here.
Hedelmone! If you'll pledge your heart to me,
Virtue and love will guide us o'er the sea.
I see her coming, followed by Hermance.


## Scene 3

### OTHELLO, HEDELMONE, HERMANCE

OTHELLO: Madam, could you be seeking me, by chance?

HEDELMONE: I need to see you, not to feed my flame;
My long-held love for you remains the same.
But I delight to have you near at hand.

OTHELLO: Madam, perhaps you'll grant me one demand?

HEDELMONE: Speak, my Othello.

OTHELLO:                          Troubles never cease.
Word of revolts threaten our fragile peace.
The Senate secretly has bid me go
Beyond the seas to subjugate the foe.
Duty and honor say I cannot wait
To give courageous service to my state.
My followers for you delay their starting.

HEDELMONE: If only we could wed before departing.

OTHELLO: I wish that too.

HEDLEMONE:                    My death I do not fear.
I'll brave tempestuous seas, if you are near.
Love laughs at danger, but another kind
Of peril occupies my anxious mind.
What if while I were gone my father died

Unreconciled to me, a parricide!
Still I have hope that all may yet go right.
The Doge is sympathetic to my plight.
If I could seek him out, and with him plead
Perhaps he would agree to intercede.

OTHELLO:          Can you be unaware this very day
A bold seducer marked you as his prey?

HEDELMONE:       Surely you won't refuse what I implore
Allow some time, I will not ask for more.

OTHELLO:          Pardon if I ...

HEDELMONE:                              Allow this one demand
Upon your love. I'm sure you understand.

OTHELLO:          It's difficult, You do not realize
What charms you have in other people's eyes.
Who knows ... perhaps ...

HERMANCE:                              What passions she may stir
She knows not, beauty is no pride for her.
But you, have you forgotten you alone
Have won her heart and love? It is your own.
What further proofs of love would she deny you?
May these, Othello, always satisfy you.
If ever some suspicion were allowed
Upon her virtuous soul to cast a cloud,
Believe her vows, allow no circumstance
To compromise your love.

OTHELLO:                              Enough, Hermance.
Perhaps I am mistaken or unfair.
But I know Venice; there one must take care.

HEDELMONE (*weeping and turning her face aside*): Alas!

HERMANCE (*aside*): Poor soul. Her suffering is great.
          (*aloud*): Your hesitation puts her in this state.
          Is it by doubts like these your love is shown?

HEDELMONE:       Hermance ...

HERMANCE:                              She pales.

HEDELMONE (*falling into an armchair*):          I faint.

OTHELLO:                        My Hedelmone!

HERMANCE:    My Lord, it is with you she's cast her fate.
Be her support, her father, and her mate.
See her compliance written on her brow.
She has forgotten all offenses now.
On you alone her loving glance is cast.

HEDELMONE:    If I were angry with you, that is past.
I've done no deed for which I might be blamed
Rather than that ...

OTHELLO:            No more! I am ashamed.
(*throwing himself at* HEDELMONE's *feet*)
Strike me. I' am unworthy of your tears.
We meet once more and I arouse your fears.
Blame me for when my foolish passion reigns,
Africa's blood still rages in my veins.
Pour on my troubled soul your virtuous balm
As at your feet I kneel and beg for calm.
Be all to me, my guiding star at night,
The air I breathe, the sun that gives me light.
May my suspicious soul be soothed to rest
By your love calmed and by your virtue blest.
(*rising*) Tomorrow, as the dawn reveals its face
Go find the Doge, and plead your father's case.
(*to* HERMANCE, *pointing to* HEDELMONE)
Watch over her, Hermance, and take her part.
If she is happy, you'll be near my heart.
If I should ever harm her with suspicion,
My Heaven cast me down to my perdition
And wrest from me as an unworthy mate
The greatest treasure given me by Fate!

HEDELMONE:    My dear Othello, go, with heart secure
Knowing my love is yours, and will endure.
I offer Heaven my heart in recompense
If ever I should cause my love offense.

*She leaves with* HERMANCE.

## Scene 4

### OTHELLO *alone.*

OTHELLO:    Nothing I know in Nature can compare
With the pure virtue I've discovered there.
This virtue needs no altar for security
But charms all mortals with its simple purity.
Unhappy he who in his insolence
Poses some challenge to its innocence!
Were my hot blood to sense such foul design,
His villainous flank would feel this blade of mine.
But now, with heavy steps Pezare appears
With mournful looks and half-suppressèd tears.

## Scene 5

### OTHELLO, PEZARE

PEZARE:    Friend, can you suffer?

OTHELLO:                                Speak.

PEZARE:                                        And can you bear
With calmness news to drive one to despair?

OTHELLO:    I am a man.

PEZARE:                            So much the worse for you.
Your Hedelmone is ...

OTHELLO:                            In a word?

PEZARE:                                        Untrue.

OTHELLO:    Untrue? What is your proof? That I must see!

PEZARE:    My proof? Why take this angry tone with me?
Who else would bear your violence untamed?
I have avenged you, and for that I'm blamed!
I met your unknown rival and I knew
At once he was the one who'd challenged you.
As soon as he had seen me anger filled him.
A brutal combat followed, and I killed him.

And from his bloody corpse this note I tore.
And this headband your Hedelmone once wore.

OTHELLO (*looking at the headband and the letter*):
I see it, and this letter gives validity
Were anymore desired, of her perfidity.

PEZARE: Read it.

OTHELLO (*reading*): "I'm guilty, father, on all counts.
This marriage with Othello I renounce!
Your patience I will never more abuse
And I will marry anyone you choose."
"Hedelmone." There it is.

PEZARE:                                   You must despise
This criminal and her outrageous lies.
But rage or hatred you do not reveal.

OTHELLO (*with the greatest calm*):
My friend, despair is all that I can feel.
My time is short. I have some obligation
To satisfy my duties to the nation.
It needs a warrior strong to carry through
The campaigns I have started. That is you.
I'll tell the Senate you must lead the fight.

PEZARE: What, I?

OTHELLO:                       After my death it is but right.
Listen. To an old man I've caused much grief.
Now in repentance I'll bring him relief.
His heart is broken; his despair is great.
He's fled. Find him and save him from his fate.
He is the only being that I know
That I have by my actions brought to woe.
My death will his familial peace restore.
Give him his daughter's letter, and what's more,
This headband:
(*He holds out both but without giving them up.*)
But say nothing of my fate.
Nothing about my life or death relate.
And may she find a more illustrious spouse
And found with him a firm and happy house.
My peace I'll find somewhere on death's dark strand.
(*He prepares to give up the letter and the headband.*)
(*with great fury*):

> Here, take this letter and this cursed band ...
> In that vile blood, that's caused me such great pain,
> I'd plunge them both, then plunge them in again.
> Where is her lover? Guide me to him, friend.
> I'll feast my eyes on his impious end.
> What joy 'twould be should she be there as well,
> I'd see upon his corpse her bosom swell;
> I'd count her sighs, then give her her reward,
> Uniting them with my avenging sword!
> (*stopping himself*) Othello, stop this barbarous display.
> Your passion blinds you, leads your steps astray.
> Never, in the most savage raids you've made
> Has any woman's blood yet stained your blade.
> The fury in myself that I detect
> Has by its very access, vengeance checked.
> Recall those words that her departing sire
> Flung in my face, as he took leave in ire:
> "Look to her, Moor, if you have eyes to see,
> She has deceived her father, and may thee."

PEZARE:      'Twas truly said.

OTHELLO:               What arts did she employ
To make her eyes deceive, her tears decoy?
Could she be true and all these charges lies?

PEZARE:      Headband and letter argue otherwise.

OTHELLO:     Had I back to my desert homeland flown
And died there, unbelovéd and unknown.

PEZARE:      I feel for you.

OTHELLO:               The rising wind, my friend
Predicts to us that tempests may impend.
Lightning forecasts that thunder is a-borning;
The lions of the desert roar their warning.
But women please and make their prey unwary
Of hidden, deadly weapons that they carry.
My Hedelmone!

PEZARE:               That name! How can you bear it?

OTHELLO:     From my expiring heart I cannot tear it!

Scene 6

OTHELLO, PEZARE, HEDELMONE

HEDELMONE:    Your cries, Othello, reached my ears and made
Me fearful. I have come to give you aid.
What ails you?

OTHELLO:                Nothing.

HEDELMONE:                Why attempt to hide?
Your heart to my heart surely can confide!

OTHELLO:    No. What you say a sympathy reveals
And what you say reflects what your heart feels.

HEDELMONE:    Why is your voice so weak?

OTHELLO:                I've been much stressed.
My body and my soul demand some rest.
I need a long repose.

HEDELMONE:                Pezare, what healing
Is needed for the pain that he is feeling?
Whence comes it? ... How? ...

OTHELLO:                Your pity I respect.

HEDELMONE:    Alas, what can I do? Heaven, protect
His soul! Sleep cure his heart!

OTHELLO:                Your heart I know
Is innocent, untouched by any woe.

*At this moment,* HEDELMONE, *who has not yet closely observed* OTHELLO, *looks at him and seeing a frightful smile upon his lips, kisses his head, trembling.*

OTHELLO:    Let's go, Pezare.

*He leaves with* PEZARE.

## Scene 7

### HEDELMONE *alone.*

HEDELMONE:    Great heavens! How he smiled,
His voice was altered and his words were wild!
What storm within his heart do these things show?
But mine is pure, and he loves me, I know.
Sooner or later all will be revealed;
He or Pezare will say what's been concealed.
Heaven, if for some sacrifice you call
On me alone let your dark edict fall!
I stand here ready, joyfully to give
My life if that allows my love to live.

## ACT V

*The stage represents* HEDELMONE's *bedchamber. Within it is a curtained bed, a lighted lamp, a few pieces of furniture, and a theorbo or ancient guitar on an armchair.*

### Scene 1

### HEDELMONE *alone.*

HEDELMONE: My eyelids close in sleep, vainly I try
To bring my father's home before my eye.
I am alone, oh Heaven, and afraid;
Thoughts of my love no longer bring me aid.
A dark foreboding on my spirits falls
Within this mournful chamber's gloomy walls.
A sudden trembling seizes me as though
From here I never more could freely go.
Why do I feel so anguished, so forsaken?
Can I, so young, by death be overtaken?
(*with a sudden and involuntary shudder*)
Who comes here?

### Scene 2

### HEDELMONE, HERMANCE

HERMANCE:                               It is I. Why this alarm?
Fear you Othello means you unjust harm?

HEDELMONE: I fear him not. I love him.

HERMANCE:                             But he spoke
In words that your misgivings might evoke.

HEDELMONE: Alas, he spoke to me of calm repose,
Of peaceful slumber, and an end to woes.
I can't explain exactly what he meant.

HERMANCE: But in his eyes could you read his intent?

HEDELMONE: His eyes one moment fixed on me alone.
He gave a smile that chilled me to the bone.

HERMANCE: What caused him to reveal this darker side?

HEDELMONE (*with profound melancholy*): The day approaches when my
        mother died.

HERMANCE:     Why dwell on matters causing you such pain?

HEDELMONE:    Within this chamber, I see hers again.

HERMANCE:     Perhaps ...

HEDELMONE:               A fatal lamp stood by her bed
O'erturned. Its lesser light had also fled.
(*regarding the lamp*) I seem to see it still.

HERMANCE:     You're overwrought.

HEDELMONE:    Of death approaching, mother never thought.

HERMANCE:     It's Heaven's wish that we not think of death
From blissful childhood 'til our final breath.

HEDELMONE:    But can you not lay out, if I implore,
The final garments that my mother wore?

HERMANCE:     If possible, put these dark thoughts aside.

HEDELMONE:    "You'll die unhappy." With those words she died.

HERMANCE:     Madame ...

HEDELMONE:              All's finished.

HERMANCE:                   In our hardest hours
Heaven brightens the thorny path with flowers.
Upon those hopeful promises rely.

HEDELMONE (*with a cry of hopelessness and terror*):
        "My dearest child, unhappy you will die."

HERMANCE:     What do I hear? You make my blood congeal.
Why such excessive panic do you feel?

HEDELMONE (*more softly*): Could my Othello, if his loving wife
        Set loose his fury, take away her life?

HERMANCE:     I fear for you. He's angry and he's jealous.

HEDELMONE:    He never has been cruel.

HERMANCE:               But he is zealous.
You walk upon a precipice, I fear.

HEDELMONE:    I can't believe his love would disappear.

HERMANCE:    Once doubts set in, then there is no return.

HEDELMONE:    Love then gets plaudits which it does not earn!

HERMANCE:    It often spawns unhappiness and crime.

HEDELMONE:    As with young Isaure, once upon a time.
Unhappy Isaure, happy 'til the day
Blind jealousy forced her true love away.
Beneath a willow she let fall her tears
And told her woes to Nature's gentle ears.
In plaintive song combining words and weeping,
She let pour out the anguish she was keeping.
I feel the need to sing her song again.
(*after a silence*) Alas! She's dead, but yet her sorrows
remain.
(*She points to the guitar on the armchair.*)
You see this instrument, silent too long?
To its strange, haunting sounds I'll join her song.

HERMANCE:    'Twill make you sadder.

HEDELMONE:               No, 'tis for my pleasure.
In solitude, its soothing notes I treasure.
We are alone, list to this song of grief
Retelling it will bring my heart relief.

I.
At the foot of the willow, Isaure lay crying
And seeing her false-hearted lover approach,
"You have wronged me," she cried, in a tearful reproach,
"Though I love you, you spurned me, and now I lay dying."
Sing willow and all its green hangings.

II.
"Like a flower, mine was an ephemeral fate
I loved ... and I died. Thus my pure soul was taken.
You'll discover in sorrow that you were mistaken
You'll discover your fault, but it will be too late."
Sing willow and all its green hangings.

III.
"The day is dying, Nature's outline blurs.
I hear the night-bird's melancholy call;
A verdant darkness settles over all.
The willow weeps, and my tears blend with hers."
Sing willow and all its green hangings.

IV.
Now night is fallen. In that darkness long
All is as dead, with empty silence filled.
The wind stirs not, the murmuring brook is stilled,
And nevermore is heard Isaure's song.
Sing willow and all its green hangings.

*The wind is heard.*

HEDELMONE (*suddenly trembling*): What is that noise?

HERMANCE:                                              'Tis wind, the
          shutters shaking.

HEDELMONE:    The night is threatening. A storm is breaking.

HERMANCE (*urgently and with growing concern*): Madam, let us depart.
          My worries grow.
          Heaven I feel is warning us to go.

HEDELMONE:    No, 'tis against my duty. I will stay.

HERMANCE:     Follow my steps, dear Hedelmone. Away!

HEDELMONE:    Where could I hide? What place have you devised?
          My father gone, my virtue compromised?

HERMANCE:     Forget your errors, cleanse them with repentance.

HEDELMONE:    But I do not yet know Othello's sentence.
          If he is jealous, he will track my path
          And if I fly, that will engage his wrath.
          Go, try to taste the soothing charms of sleep.

HERMANCE:     In leaving you, I cannot help but weep.

HEDELMONE:    I wish it.

HERMANCE:           Then I take my leave of you.
          My daughter ... child ...

HEDELMONE: My dear Hermance, adieu.

HERMANCE *goes.*


## Scene 3

### HEDELMONE *alone.*

HEDELMONE: Her tender love my mother's does recall.
(*She kneels beside her bed.*)
Heavenly father, watching over all,
Calm my own father, grant that I once more
Can stroke his white locks, as I did before.
Remove suspicions from my dear Othello,
Speak through his friend Pezare, that virtuous fellow.
Show that unfailing mercy you accord
To all unhappy mortals, gracious Lord.
My errors I confess, your mercy seek,
Spare Hedelmone, too feeble and too weak.
(*She lies on the bed.*)
But conquering sleep now breeches my defenses
And overtakes my spirit and my senses.
Its cool, refreshing calm spreads through my veins,
Knits up my wounds, and soothes away my pains.
Sleep, bring into my heart your soft repose
And let my eyes in your sweet comfort close.

*She lowers her head and sleeps.*


## Scene 4

### HEDELMONE *sleeping,* OTHELLO.

OTHELLO: Restrain yourself. Let not your passionate soul
Lead you too far. Retain your self-control.
She must not die ... The somber lighting here
Still shows that beauty that I still hold dear.
(*He regards the illumination from the lamp.*)
Ah, were I to extinguish this small flame,
I could relight it; it would be the same.
(*He looks at* HELDEMONDE.)
But if this mortal flame, now softly burning
I should put out, there would be no returning.
What purity in her soft breaths I hear,
Her powerful charms as always draw me near.

Subside, my blood, that overwhelms my sense
Eager once more to rise in your defense.
In dark retreats like this one, many times
Venice has drowned its criminals and crimes.
Without complaint, without a hope of grace
I could have dragged my life out in this place.
But worse to see the horror here displayed,
My tenderness, my honor so betrayed.
See how perfidiously this tender brow
No hint of its betrayal will allow.
But on this perjury I've dwelt too long,
My suffering is great, as is my wrong.
Put all but death aside.

HEDELMONE: What do I see?
Othello, is it you?

OTHELLO: Yes, peaceful be.

HEDELMONE: You startled me. Forgive my troubled state.
What brings you to this quiet retreat so late?

OTHELLO: I come to you with agitated mind
In hopes that peace and calm I here will find.

HEDELMONE: And to what trouble can I bring relief?

OTHELLO: Love often carries in its wake some grief.

HEDELMONE: Doubt you my heart?

OTHELLO: Me! ... No.

HEDELMONE: You hesitate!

OTHELLO: My love!

HEDELMONE: Othello!

OTHELLO (*aside*): What to tell her?

HEDELMONE: Wait!
Perhaps, my dear, you've noticed that the band
Is gone, that tribute from your loving hand.
I wanted it not used for idle show
But to support my father in his woe.
A young man took it, father's name to clear.

OTHELLO:          What young man?

HEDELMONE:                    Loredan.

OTHELLO (*aside*):                        What secret's here?
                   (*aloud*) The Doge's son! My jealousy's removed.
                   This young man you've met but never loved?

HEDELMONE:        Never, I swear.

OTHELLO:                            But maybe he loves you?

HEDELMONE:        I've told him that's a path he can't pursue.

OTHELLO:          But if he as my rival should appear?

HEDELMONE:        Othello, it's you alone that I hold dear.

OTHELLO:          You love me then?

HEDELMONE:                            Hear this. Nature has sent
                   Imposters to eternal punishment.
                   If I've deceived you, let my guilty eyes
                   Read condemnation written in the skies!
                   May Heaven's wrath prevent this suffering child
                   From being with her father reconciled.
                   Are you content?

OTHELLO:                            I am! And all you've said
                   Is Just. Your father's wrath be on your head
                   Along with Heaven's. Nature has never known
                   Duplicity more heinous than your own.
                   A heart that makes all vows and oaths a jest
                   Of all crimes capable, by none distressed.

HEDELMONE:        Ah God! Can I in such terms be accused?

OTHELLO:          Here, read this letter. Have you been abused?
                   You know this hand?

HEDELMONE:                            My courage fades away ...

OTHELLO:          Of virtue now, what can you dare to say?
                   What cunning mischief can you now invent?
                   Read.

HEDELMONE:            Heaven!

OTHELLO:                              Read. This is your punishment.
              Read.

HEDEMONE:              "I am guilty, father, on all counts.
              This marriage with Othello I renounce!
              Your patience I will never more abuse
              And I will marry anyone you choose."
              "Hedelmone."

OTHELLO:                              Can you offer some reply?

HEDELMON:    Against me all conspires.

OTHELLO:                              And proves you lie.
              (*suddenly changing both his voice and expression*)
              Look at me now. What do you gaze upon?

HEDELMONE:    Husband and lover both, I see, are gone.
              'Tis death I see. Dear father, you were right.

OTHELLO:    Before you journey into endless night
              From God remains there anything to ask?

HEDELMONE:    I'd pray for you.

OTHELLO:                              I'll leave you to your task.
              Do not be long.

*He walks about.*

HEDELMONE:                              What should I say, my Lord?

OTHELLO:    Prepare yourself.

HEDELMONE:                      For what?

OTHELLO (*drawing his sword*):              For your reward.

HEDELMONE (*crying out*):                              Help me,
              oh God!

OTHELLO:              Silence, prepare to die.
              Think on your soul.

HEDELMONE:                      Upon my knees I cry,
              Othello!

OTHELLO: Death!

HELDEMONE: Still, dying I declare
That never ...

OTHELLO (*with the greatest tenderness*) If you're innocent, I swear
My every drop of blood I'd give for you.
(*with a calm and cold fury*) This Loredan ...

HEDELMONE: Still loves me, it is true.

OTHELLO (*aside*): Oh torment! (*aloud*) Answer me, why did you write
That you renounce my hand? Surely you might
Still have some hope of reconciliation.

HEDELMONE: My father came in greatest agitation:
"Come sign this letter, sign, or I will use
This dagger!" were his words. Could I refuse?
I signed.

OTHELLO: And read it not?

HEDELMONE: No. All was planned.
Loredan seized the moment and my hand.
I raised my protests, father's rage increased ...
Hear me! You doubt my word!

OTHELLO: Not in the least.
Go on.

HEDELMONE: Moved by my protests, he became resigned
And gave me back the letter I had signed.

OTHELLO: Then?

HEDELMONE: I gave it to Loredan.

OTHELLO (*aside*): Oh rage!
Why trust my rival with that fatal page?

HEDELMONE: So that ...

OTHELLO: Go on ...

HEDELMONE: His father, now excited
By this false news of his son's marriage plighted
Would spare my father.

OTHELLO:                                  And by this affair
                    You sought to fool the Doge?

HEDELMONE:                                          By Heaven I swear
                    It is the only time I ever lied.

OTHELLO:            And Loredan ...

HEDELMONE:                        Faithfully took my side
                    Before the Doge, and by his generous deed
                    Preserved my father in his hour of need.

OTHELLO:            And without hope he came to your support?

HEDELMONE:          He did.

OTHELLO:                        You give a beautiful report.
                    But I see through his generous disguise,
                    The two of you have formed this enterprise.
                    You did not think that I'd see through your plan
                    Involving both the Doge and Loredan.
                    That's why just now when my outrage was hidden,
                    You would not leave with me as you were bidden.
                    But Heaven's punishment you won't avoid.
                    Here are the note and headband you employed.
                    (*He shows her the letter in one hand and the headband
                    in the other.*)
                    It was Pezare who just now brought them to me.

HEDELMONE:          Pezare! Your friend! A new hope rushes through me!
                    He got them then from Loredan, which proves
                    My father blesses us, our love approves!

OTHELLO:            From Loredan it's true that he received them,
                    But it was from a corpse that he relieved them.
                    Loredan, felled by twenty blows he left
                    Upon the bloody ground, of life bereft.

HEDELMONE:          He's dead! He's dead!

OTHELLO:                                  Your tears betray the truth.

HEDELMONE:          Heaven! Hear him!

OTHELLO:                                  You mourn his charm, his youth.

HEDELMONE:          Loredan! Loredan!

OTHELLO:                                     Wretch, why are you crying?

HEDELMONE:    I laud his virtue both in life and dying.
                         He's innocent.

OTHELLO:                          A traitor. I abhor him.

HEDELMONE:    He's innocent, and we should all pray for him.

OTHELLO:        See you this dagger?

HEDELMONE:                                     I've no fear of death.
                         I'll shout his innocence with my last breath.

OTHELLO:        His innocence!

HEDELMONE:                      Unto my Heavenly Lord
                         I'll swear it, by my love, e'en by your sword!

OTHELLO (*striking her with a blow of his dagger*): Die then.

HEDELMONE:    Dear God!

*She takes several steps backward and falls dead at the foot of her bed.*

OTHELLO:                                I did what I must do.
                         Her love is punished, and her crime is too.
                         Who ever could believe that one so young
                         Could coldly use such a deceiving tongue?
                         It is the climate. The corrupting air
                         Of Venice must her degradation share.
                         Should I have pitied ... No, her guilt was clear
                         The note ... the headband ... all the proof is here.
                         Her execrable boldness forced my hand.
                         My vengeance everyone will understand.
                         But I hear steps. Perhaps Pezare returns
                         To give me consolation. My soul burns.
                         A child, a woman! Pardon I must seek
                         This barbarous act has left my spirits weak,
                         (*He dares not turn his eyes toward the body of*
                         HEDELMONE.)
                         She's there! Regard. (*He looks upon her.*) Unmoving.
                         Without sense.
                         As in a tomb! ... Come, hide my foul offense.
                         (*He pulls the curtains on the bed, hiding her from the*
                         *eyes of the audience.*)
                         (*with terror*) Who comes here?

## Scene 5

### OTHELLO, HERMANCE

HERMANCE:       Lord, Pezare your backing needs.
                He's charged with the most criminal of deeds.
                The undercover agents of the state
                Have followed him and say these crimes are great.

## Scene 6

### OTHELLO, HERMANCE, MONCENIGO, LOREDAN, ODALBERT, MEN *carrying torches.*

MONCENIGO (*to* OTHELLO, *pointing out his son to him*):
                See Loredan.

OTHELLO:                              What's this?

MONCENIGO:                                     Pezare was never
                Your friend. He's been your enemy forever.
                Lusting for Hedelmone, he, by dark art
                Disguised his projects, working on your heart.
                Pretending in your projects to support you
                Before the very altar he would thwart you.
                He stirred your flames by cleverly creating
                A ruthless rival you'd be sure of hating.
                Upon whose person he'd claim to discover
                A letter and the headband of your lover.
                Alas! My son believed him your true friend
                And so, in secret, trusted him to rend
                To Hedelmone alone this band and better
                That forced, false, incriminating letter.
                Pezare, that monster, saw that he could use
                These items in his campaign to abuse
                Your confidence and drive you to such deeds
                As would destroy you and fulfill his needs.
                Much of this plot already he's confessed
                And our best tortures will expose the rest.
                (*He indicates his son.*) Here is your rival.

LOREDAN (*to* OTHELLO): Yes, and your defenses
                I've made, and brought her father to his senses.
                The Senate now regards his anger clearly
                As not against authority but merely

> A father's understandable dismay
> At losing his lone daughter in this way.
> Othello, you have gained your love at last;
> Her father's opposition now is past.
> Live happy and thank Heaven which has spared
> You from the trap your enemy prepared.

OTHELLO (*distracted, having heard nothing of this*): What have you said?

LOREDAN: Speak.

HERMANCE: Why do you ignore us?
What's this?

ODALBERT: My child! Why is she not before us?

OTHELLO: She's sleeping now. In quiet let her be.

HERMANCE *drawing the bed-curtains. The dead body of* HEDELMONE *is seen and the blood from her wound.* HERMANCE *runs toward the bed.*

HERMANCE: Oh Heaven. I see all!

OTHELLO: Where can I flee?
My Hedelmone!

MONCENIGO: Ah, what a fearful sight!

OTHELLO: Such charms ... such virtues ... May the Heaven's might
Fall on me. Dead!

ODALBERT: In this I played my part.

OTHELLO: Dead! Dead! And it was I who stopped her heart!
(*looking at her*) Gentle and tender victim. Loving wife.
Gone now for ever. Take from me this life.
My wife ... my friends, oh, pity me my woe.
(*He clasps her in his arms.*)
One last embrace! Now, joining her, I go.

*He stabs himself and dies beside her.*

*The curtain falls.*

**HAPPY ENDING** *which may be substituted for the tragic one.*
*The changes begin in the middle of* scene 4 *of* ACT V.

OTHELLO:      See you this dagger?

HEDELMONE:                      I've no fear of death.
I'll shout his innocence with my last breath.

OTHELLO:      His innocence!

HEDELMONE:                Unto my Heavenly Lord
I'll swear it, by my love, e'en by your sword!

OTHELLO (*raising his sword and preparing to strike her*):
Then for your crimes ...



## Scene 5

OTHELLO, HERMANCE, MONCENIGO, LOREDAN, ODALBERT, MEN *carrying torches*.

MONCENIGO (*seizing the sword*):        Barbarian, hold back!
What could possess you virtue to attack?
(*pointing to his son*)
Cruel one. See Loredan.

HEDELMONE:                  Speak now. Discover.
Am I an innocent or guilty lover?

OTHELLO (*to* HEDELMONE): What should I do? What choices face me?
Must I not seek revenge?

HEDELMONE:                  My love, embrace me!

LOREDAN:      Othello, as you see, she pardons you.
It's to your rival that your thanks are due.

OTHELLO:      My rival!

LOREDAN:           That is me, my friend. Alas!
Pezare's dark plottings brought us to this pass.
Lusting for Hedelmone, he, by dark art
Disguised his projects, working on your heart.
Pretending in your projects to support you
Before the very altar he would thwart you.

|  |  |
|---|---|
|  | He stirred your flames by cleverly creating |
|  | A ruthless rival you'd be sure of hating. |
|  | Upon whose person he'd claim to discover |
|  | A letter and the headband of your lover. |
| MONCENIGO: | Alas! My son believed him your true friend |
|  | And so, in secret, trusted him to rend |
|  | To Hedelmone alone this band and better |
|  | That forced, false, incriminating letter. |
|  | Pezare, that monster, saw that he could use |
|  | These items in his campaign to abuse |
|  | Your confidence and drive you to such deeds |
|  | As would destroy you and fulfill his needs. |
|  | Threatened with torture, this perfidious one |
|  | Confessed all the dark deeds that he had done. |
|  | Live, brave Othello. Loredan's defense |
|  | Of you brought Odalbert at last to sense. |
|  | The Senate now regards his anger clearly |
|  | As not against authority but merely |
|  | A father's understandable dismay |
|  | At losing his lone daughter in this way. |
|  | Your match with Hedelmone I here endorse. |
| ODALBERT: | And know you now have my support, of course. |
|  | Othello, on my love you can rely. |
|  | Become my son, and my most close ally. |
|  | Along with Venice, I your nuptials bless |
|  | To you I trust my daughter's happiness. |
| OTHELLO: | Thus all the evil deeds that I've committed |
|  | Toward each of you, you've graciously remitted |
|  | With benefits. How can I e'er repay |
|  | The virtues you have shown to me today? |
|  | My heart, whose darkness I can scarcely face, |
|  | Can it be worth your love and Heaven's grace? |
|  | (to LOREDAN) Oh noble rival! (to ODALBERT) Father now most dear! |
|  | I scarcely dare behold you both so near. |
|  | (to HEDELMONE) And you, whom I almost deprived of life, |
|  | Can you forgive my crime, become my wife? |
| HEDELMONE: | Already it's forgotten. I'll not cease |
|  | Working to bring your troubled heart to peace. |

OTHELLO (to HEDELMONE): Pezare's betrayal still will cause me pain.

MONCENIGO:     In Venice's dark cells he will remain.
               Should you decide his perfidy requires
               His death, you need but mention your desires.

OTHELLO:       So many goodnesses I have received
               I too must pardon where I've been deceived.
               As if reborn, I'll now devote my life
               To serve my fatherland and love my wife.
               Oh, God, the sacred name of husband given,
               Let me acquit myself toward her and Heaven.
               Let me deserve the gifts you have bestowed
               And all that is to the Republic owed.
               May my strong arm preserve her if I may
               Or give me death amidst the battle's fray.

*The curtain falls.*

## NOTE ON THE EDITOR AND TRANSLATOR

MARVIN CARLSON is the Sidney E. Cohn Professor of Theatre, Comparative Literature, and Middle Eastern Studies at the Graduate Center of the City University of New York. He has previously translated plays from French, German, Italian, and Arabic and is the author of many books and articles on theatre and performance history and theory. He has edited in this series *The Arab Oedipus: Four Plays* (2005) and *Four Plays from North Africa* (2008).

The **Martin E. Segal Theatre Center (MESTC)** is a non-profit center for theatre, dance, and film affiliated with CUNY's PhD Program in Theatre. The Center's mission is to bridge the gap between academia and the professional performing arts communities both within the United States and internationally. By providing an open environment for the development of educational, community-driven, and professional projects in the performing arts, **MESTC** is a home to theatre scholars, students, playwrights, actors, dancers, directors, dramaturgs, and performing arts managers from the local and international theatre communities.

Through diverse programming—staged readings, theatre events, panel discussions, lectures, conferences, film screenings, dance—and a number of publications, **MESTC** enables artists, academics, visiting scholars, and performing arts professionals to participate actively in the advancement and appreciation of the entire range of theatrical experience. The Center presents staged readings to further the development of new and classic plays, lecture series, televised seminars featuring professional and academic luminaries, and arts in education programs, and maintains its long-standing visiting scholars-from-abroad program. In addition, the Center publishes a series of highly-regarded academic journals, as well as books, including plays in translation, written, translated, and edited by leading scholars. www.theSegalCenter.org

The PhD Program in Theatre, The Graduate Center, CUNY, is one of the leading doctoral theatre programs in the United States. The Faculty includes distinguished professors, holders of endowed chairs, and internationally recognized scholars. The program trains future scholars and teachers in all the disciplines of theatre research. Faculty members edit **MESTC** publications, working closely with the doctoral students in theatre who perform a variety of editorial functions and learn the skills involved in the creation of books and journals. www.web.gc.cuny.edu/theatre.org.

The **MESTC** Publication Wing produces both journals and individual volumes. Journals include *Slavic and Eastern European Performance* (*SEEP*), *The Journal of American Drama and Theatre* (*JADT*), and *Western European Stages* (*WES*). Books include *Four Melodramas by Pixérécourt* (edited by Daniel Gerould and Marvin Carlson—both Distinguished Professors of Theatre at the CUNY Graduate Center), *Contemporary Theatre in Egypt*, *The Heirs of Moliere* (edited and translated by Marvin Carlson), *Seven Plays by Stanisław Ignacy Witkiewicz* (edited and translated by Daniel Gerould), *The Arab Oedipus: Four Plays* (edited by Marvin Carlson), *Theatre Research Resources in New York City* (edited by Jessica Brater, Senior Editor Marvin Carlson), and *Comedy: A Bibliography of Critical Studies in English on the Theory and Practice of Comedy in Drama, Theatre and Performance* (edited by Meghan Duffy, Senior Editor Daniel Gerould).
New publications include: *BAiT-Buenos Aires in Translation: Four Plays* (edited and translated by Jean Graham-Jones), *roMANIA AFTER 2000: Five New Romanian Plays* (edited by Saviana Stanescu and Daniel Gerould), *Four Plays from North Africa* (edited by Marvin Carlson), *Barcelona Plays: A Collection of New Plays by Catalan Playwrights* (edited and translated by Marion Peter Holt and Sharon G. Feldman), *Czech Plays: Seven New Works* (edited by Marcy Arlin, Gwynn MacDonald and Daniel Gerould), *Playwrights before the Fall* (edited by Daniel Gerould), *Timbre4* (edited and translated by Jean Graham-Jones), *Jan Fabre: The Servant of Beauty* and *I Am a Mistake* (edited and foreword by Frank Hentschker).

IN MEMORIUM: Daniel Gerould *( 1928-2012), MESTC Director of Publications